Sana Teaching Painting and Drawing
(applying the simplest technique) Volume 1

Author : mohammad manochehri

Cover by : maryam alsadat anjam

ISBN : 978-1939123947

Publisher : Supreme Century

No. of Pages : 108

@Sana1art

WWW.ART-SANA.COM

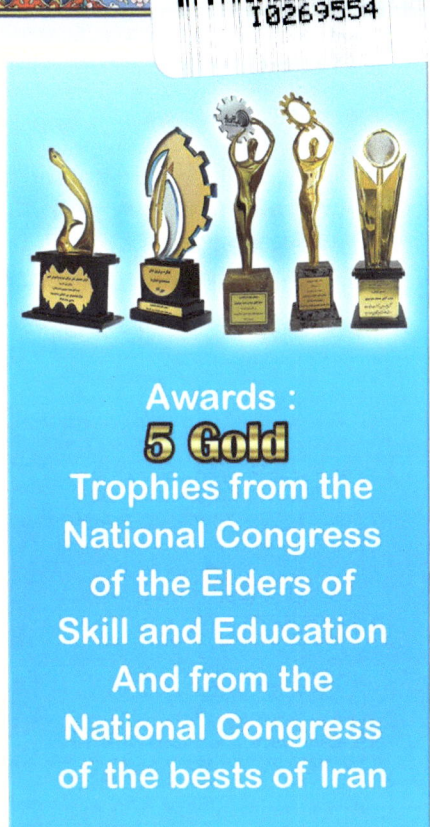

Awards:
5 Gold
Trophies from the National Congress of the Elders of Skill and Education And from the National Congress of the bests of Iran

In the name of God

Introduction

The ability to do something fast and carefully is called skill while art is creativity and innovation in every skill which is in the path of perfection! Therefore, the prerequisite and prior condition of art is being skillful. To motivate our children and beginners to show creativity and innovation, the new generation should be taught some special skills.

In Sana series we have tried to make learning drawing, painting, and similar skills easy through applying mathematical simplification.

From the early stage of their lives, human beings inclined to the skills of drawing and painting, but mostly the practical aspect (as a device to express concepts through visual lines), not merely decorative! Drawing is the common language of all the nations which cannot be prevented from being understood by territorial borders, language and even cultural ones! The skill (drawing) is as old as human beings. The existing drawings on the wall of caves, rocks, and stones prove the reality that human beings drew to communicate (as a visualized writing), recording daily events or even as the means for witch crafting (to instill the feeling of fighting, dominating on the nature, and hunting). Today, drawing and painting are used practically and decoratively in our daily lives. We are trying to teach the audience of the Sana Book Series the ability and skill (drawing and painting), applying simplification
(the same method used in mathematics),
accompanied with fun. The book series can be used for different age groups. We hope it will be a guide for families to improve the new generation's mind, talents, and general abilities.

A word for teachers and parents

With all due respects to all, due to lack of professional art teachers in elementary schools of Iran the skill of drawing and painting has yet to reach a reasonable standard amongst the students.
To increase the standard the teachers need to be trained. In this book we have taken steps to simplify the training of this basic and necessary field, especially for children and teenagers. The products are named SANA and the method used is the result of years of experience and teaching in different school levels and is presented as a codified method. This package and method not only focuses on teaching and creating drawing and painting skills and beautiful handwriting in children and teenagers but also provides means of growth and development of their other skills.

The purpose of SANA

1) The teachers can teach and instruct the students at a professional level in drawing, painting, collage and beautiful handwriting without having any experience in them.
2) The SANA package is designed to stimulate the minds of student thereby increasing their interest in drawing.
3) By this unique method, a close relationship is established between the hand and the brain of the student.
4) SANA teaches the students that they should have a goal in their minds and analyze that goal and then reach that target with a proper and principled.
5) SANA establishes order and discipline and helps increase focus in the students.
6) SANA will increase self-confidence and self-belief of the student.

SANA can be used to teach drawings and paintings to teenagers.

SANA can be used to teach drawings and paintings to teenagers.

1) Free Drawing and Painting.   2) Teaching.   3) Creativity.

SANA is focusing on the second item which is teaching. Although the teacher maybe aware of the knowledge and experience, but we shall introduce the methods briefly.

1) Free Drawing and Painting

In this step the student has the liberty to use his/her imagination and personal taste to draw and paint and describe his/her art . The student uses his/her emotional feelings and imagination along his/her skills to create an artifact . Therefore to complete this step , he/she needs to explain and describe his/her art to the audience .

2) Teaching

This step focuses on teaching and developing of Drawing and Painting practically and theoretically .
The teaching has made the job easy for the teachers .

3) Creativity

The purpose of this step is developing imagination, innovation and focus of the students . This can be achieved through various ways . For example , we can draw a small object like an eye and request the students to complete it or we can narrate a story or a historical event and ask them to illustrate it . We may also draw a part of a painting and ask the students to complete the painting .

All the best !

WWW.ART-SANA.COM

In this book :

Before starting any work, first we need to decide the purpose of a work so then it can be well guided and the purpose can be achieved properly. Meaning it has to be clear whether the purpose is education or not (utilizing the books and tips and tricks of Drawing and Painting and sense of perfectionism is for aggregating human's capability and talents). In addition to the above , the main purpose is developing the art of Drawing and Painting. In this book we shall try to address both .

Drawing ;

Drawing is visualizing and picturing what is in the mind, on a 2D surface whether it's reality (such as a picture of a horse) or imagination (a unicorn)
The first level in any learning any art is to know the tools and materials and to know their usage.

Here is an example :

In order to construct a building we need the help of a skilled man who is the architect. He will design the structure. We will also need a piece of land. For the architect, the land can be his papers sheets or canvas. The tools for the architects are shovel , spade…. And for drawing, the tools are pencil, eraser and drawing board etc . Then according to his knowledge and experience, the architect will give shape to the building with the help of certain formulae . We know these materials as construction materials which are actually the elements and components of the building.
In drawing , hese materials and elements are called visual elements (elements which can be understood by sight)

Visual elements in Drawing and Painting :

[3]The materials, elements and composition of a drawing or a painting are called the Visual Elements .
which are : 1) Dot .   2) Line .   3) Surface (plane shape) .   4) Volume, complex shape .
5) Perspective .   6) Composition . 7) Light (shade/light) .   8) Texture (rough/ smooth) .
9) Color .

It must be mentioned that there are more visual elements than the above but only these are suitable for the age and understanding of the student.

1) point : Dot is the smallest trace of writing and Dot is the intersection of two lines .
Dot has no dimension (length/ width / breadth) .

2) **Line** : The most prominent visual element is line and is made up of continuous dots in and order .
The route on which the dot moves is line . •←——• The border between two surface is line .

Types of lines : Lines are divided in to 2 groups straight and bent .

Straight lines :   1) Vertical line   2) Historical line : ———   3) Diagonal line

None straight :   1) Bent line   2) Curved line

Every sketch regardless of it shade, light and texture is a skillful combination of lines .

For a better perception we shall analyze a simple sketch of a boat

We shall separate the shade,   light and texture from the sketch

We shall breakdown the design into a plane

We shall breakdown the boat in to lines

    So we can see that every design is a mastered and an organized combination of various line, if ever someone achieves such level of skill to draw and combine the lines in same quality which he sees, then he has taken the biggest step towards becoming an artist . This is possible only by good observation / memorizing well and drawing it by hands. So the most important parameter in becoming an artist is to know the form and size of the lines and then performing them. (The visual element has one dimension) .

In order to draw a good line, certain joints and parts of the arm is put to work. Tiny and fine lines are drawn by the movement of the finger joints .
Medium size lines are drawn with the help of the wrist and finally long and stretched lines are drawn by the movement of the elbow and shoulder.

Surface (simple shape) : When two lines meet, we have a surface .
Surfaces are divided in to organized and unorganized groups .
Organized surfaces : They are simple shapes and surfaces
which have a certain geometrical name such as : square, triangle, circle .

Unorganized surfaces : All those which do not have a geometrical name such as :

Once the definition of line is studied and understood, the most common matter in
drawing is studying and observing surface .
A surface is a 2D (length, width) visual element. In order to master drawing,
the students must practice on even and uneven surfaces .

Volume (body) : A body is made up of appropriate combination of few surfaces .
Body has a third dimension which is depth .

Perspective : According to perspective principle, the objects will become smaller, their color will fade and they will be seen blur as they recede into the distance. Therefore as they get closer, their color becomes richer and they seem clearer. It's obligatory to follow this principle in Drawing and Painting so that the finished work shall be as similar to the reality as possible .

There are three types of perspectives. 1st point perspective, 2nd point, 3rd point..

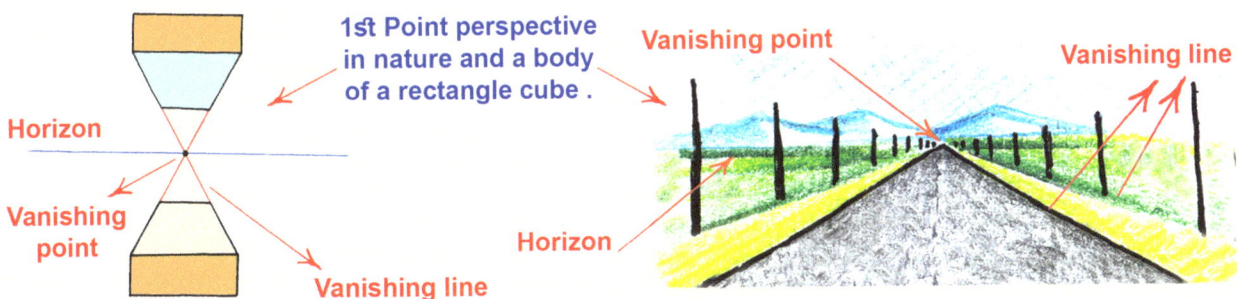

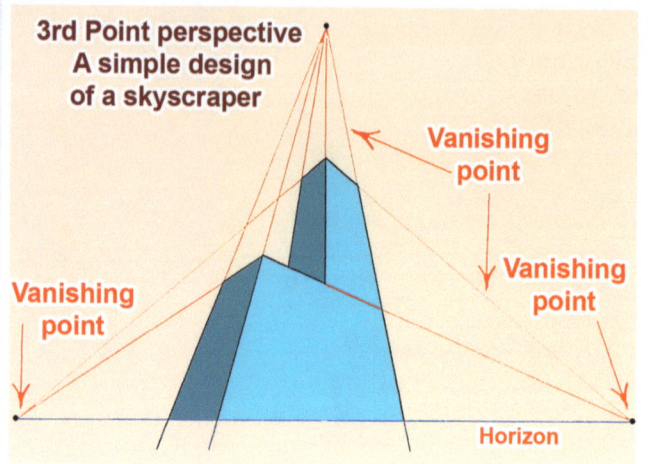
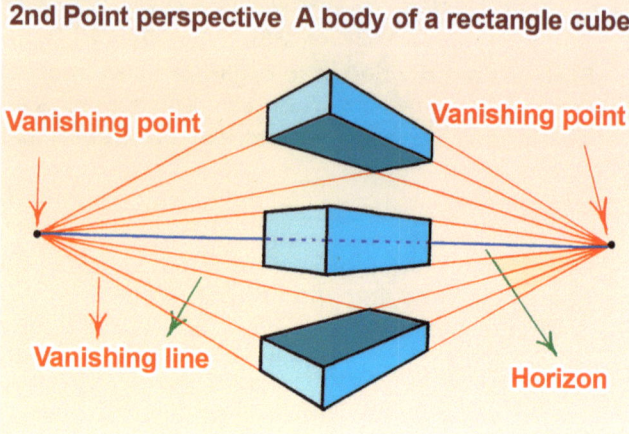

With the help of perspective we can display a 3rd image on a 2D plane, albeit by using the elements of this science :
Vanishing point Horizon Vanishing line

Vanishing point : point where parallel line meet .

Horizon : It is a line at the same level as the viewers eyes. In nature, its horizon is the apparent line that separates earth from sky . In 1 point 2 point perspective, the vanishing lines are placed on horizon ...

Vanishing line : Vanishing lines are lines which are projected from vanishing points to the viewer and the surrounding .

Composition : composition is placement of elements of a model in an appropriate frame work of art (such that the harmony , balance and the connection of the elements which are principles of composition are well taken in to notice) .

Tipos de encuadre :

Every composition requires it's unique and proper frame , which the artist / painter shall choose according to the principles criteria of composition .

- Square frame
- Horizontal rectangular frame
- Vertical rectangular frame

Frames 1,2,3 have coordinate composition and from 4 has uncoordinated composition

Vertical frame and composition - Uncoordinated

Vertical frame and composition coordinate

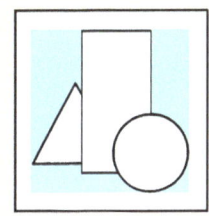
Coordinate- square frame and composition coordinate

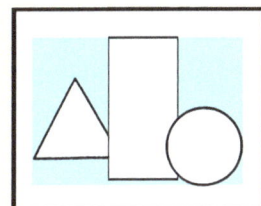
The frame and composition both horizontal- coordinate

inéquilibre

équilibre

They don't have visual relevance but they have subjective relevance

Both have visual and subjective relevance

Light (light/shadow) : If a light is projected on a model , the side that light is reflected is brighter and the other side is darker and has shadow .
The technique of showing the difference in the bright and dark sides in drawing is called shadow and light .
The light source is divided into two groups .
Natural light (sun/moon)
Artificial light (lamp, candle) . Intensity of light is categorized in two groups, direct and indirect .

shadow is categorized in two groups , shadow and cast shadow

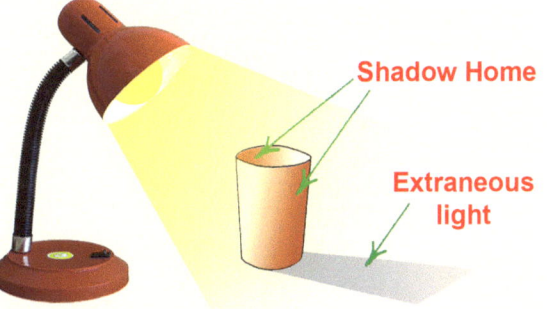

Shadow Home

Extraneous light

texture (rough and smooth) :

The outer layer is called texture . In addition to displaying the direction of light and shadow , artist should display the texture as well . For example , if light is projected on a gunny and a silk , the artist should show the shadow such that the viewer can distinguish the texture of the fabrics

Easy drawing method (simplifying in drawing) :

Like math , there are methods in drawing which can simplify drawing. The student can use his/her primary skills to develop more advanced skills. For example, in order to draw and design a complicated model, we can find simple geometrical shapes which are easy for the student to draw , then by adding more lines to them more complicated shapes can be drawn . See the sample below.

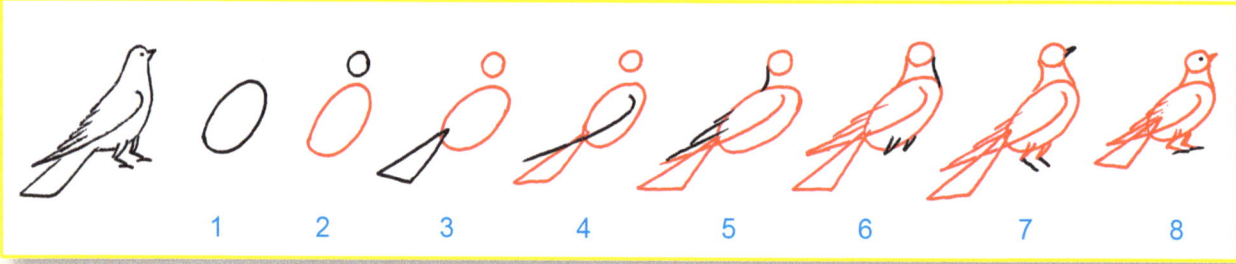

By Using this method (simplifying) complicated shapes can be drawn very easily. For this purpose , we are teaching few models and subjects so by learning this method , you can draw more easily and with more pleasure .

Take notice that the method mentioned above is not limited to Drawing and Painting.
This method is applicable to higher levels . We shall display different examples for different ages .

Please note that at each of the drawing section of the book , the new lines are in black color and the lines from previous step are in red .
Therefore the student should pay attention to the black lines and continue.

Straight lines   Curved lines

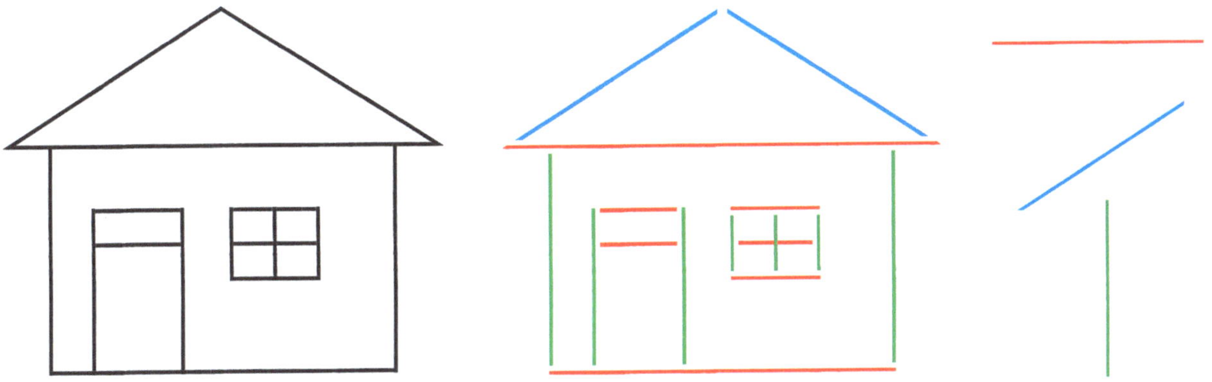

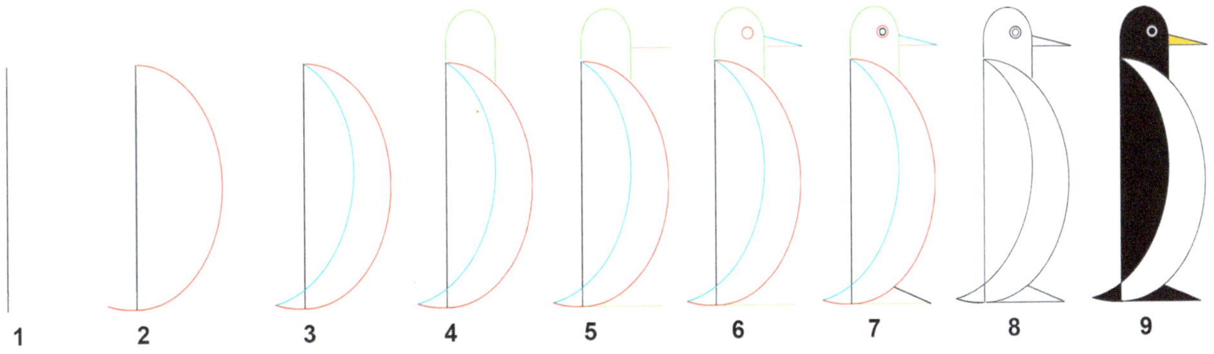

1 2 3 4 5 6 7 8 9

Düzenli Yüzeyler

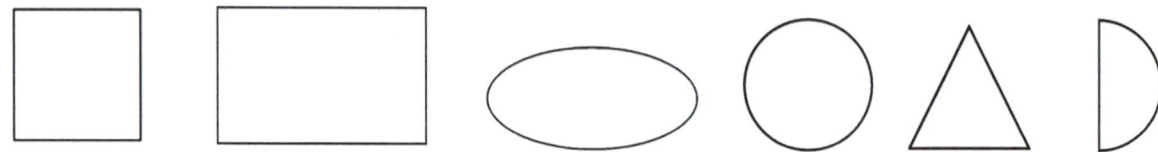

Düzensiz Yüzeyler

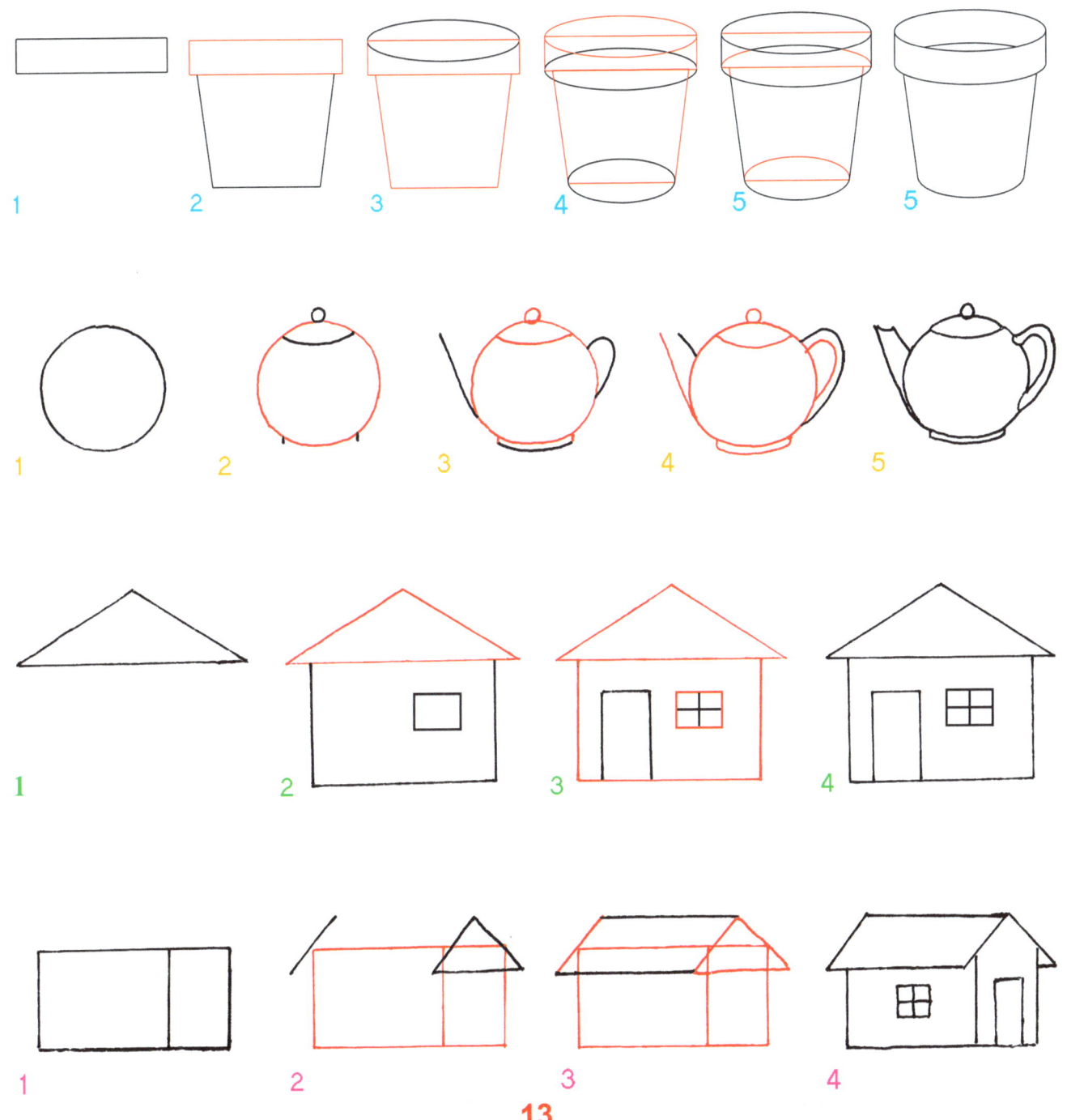

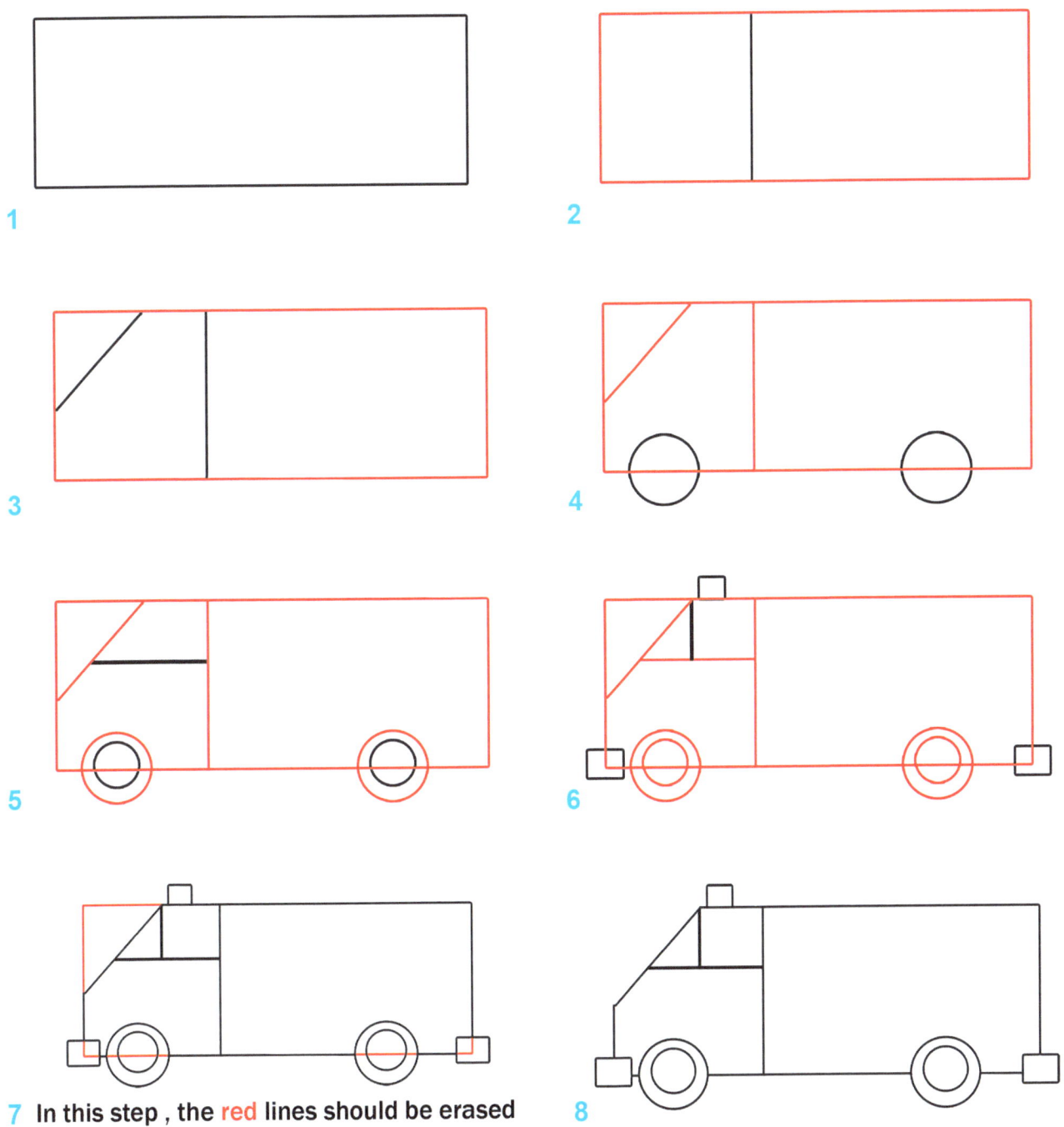

7 In this step, the red lines should be erased

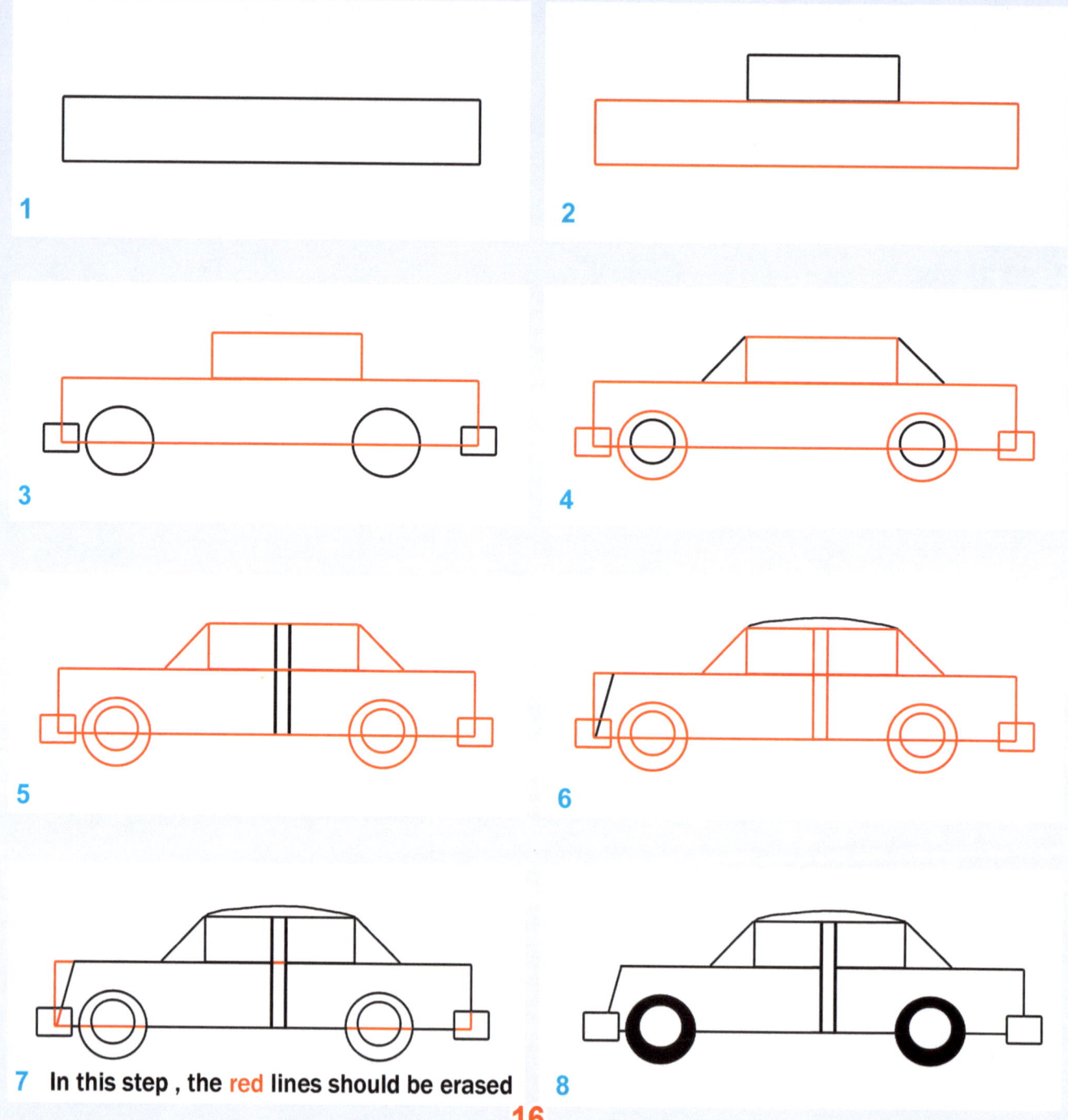

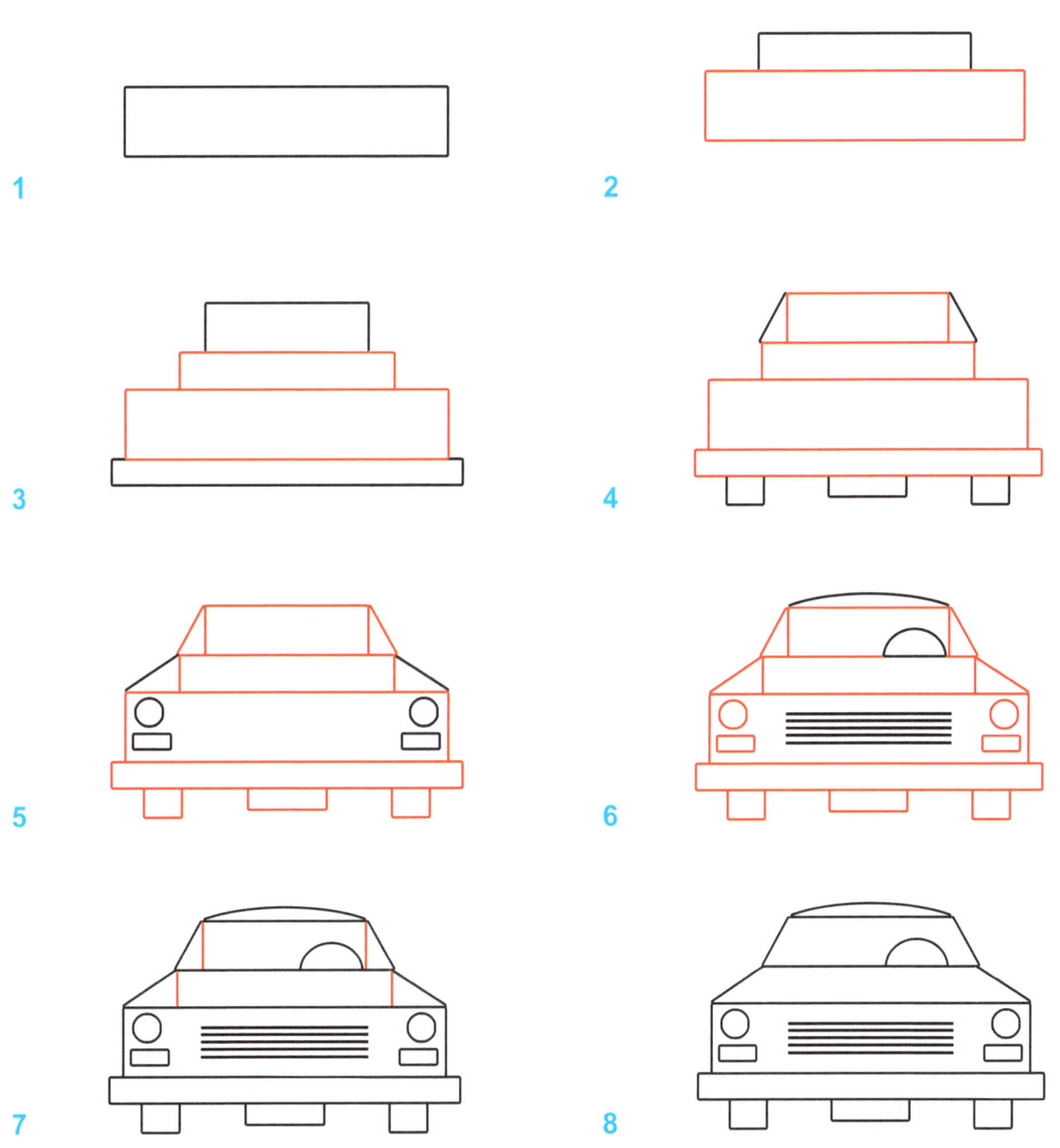

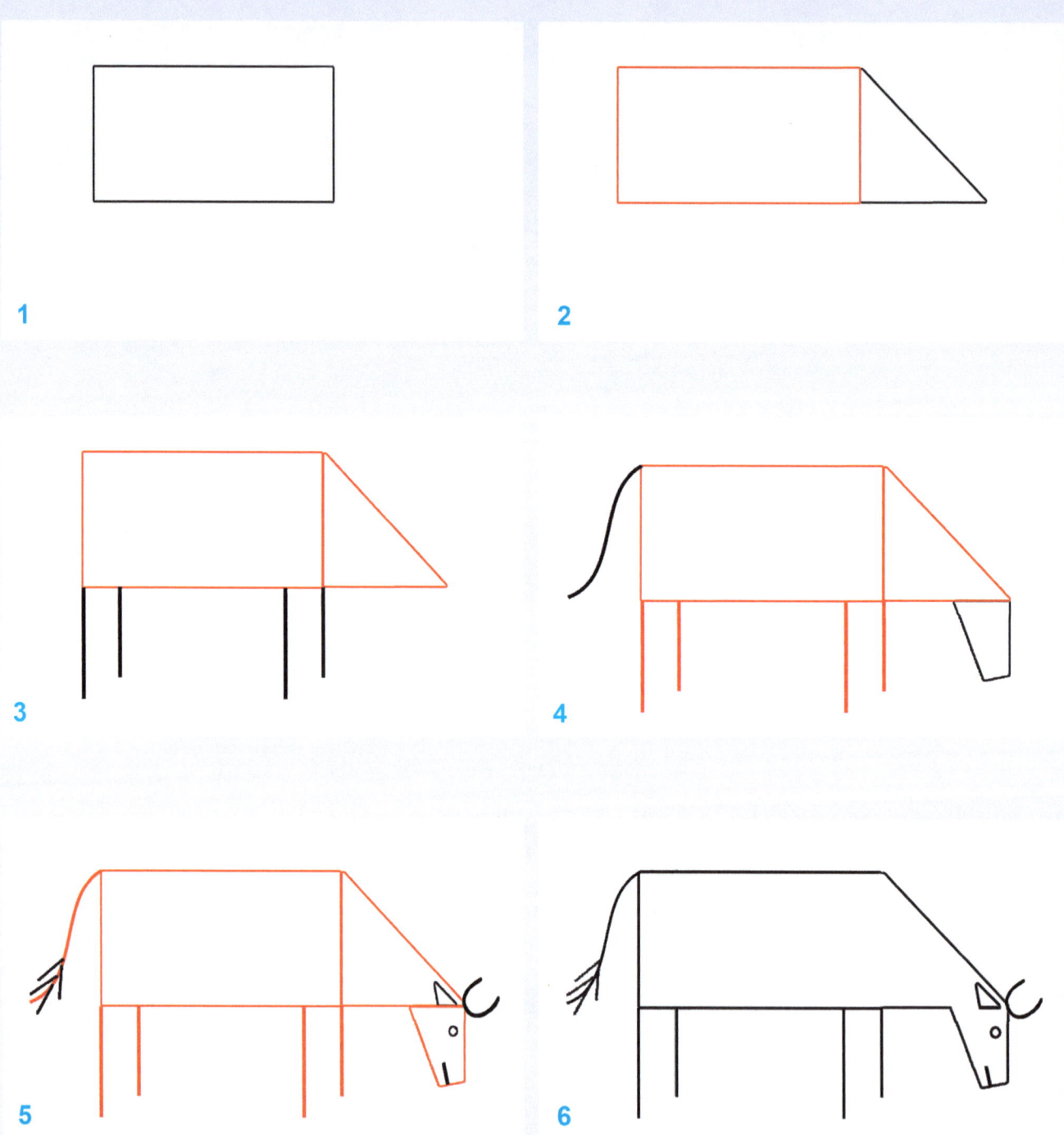

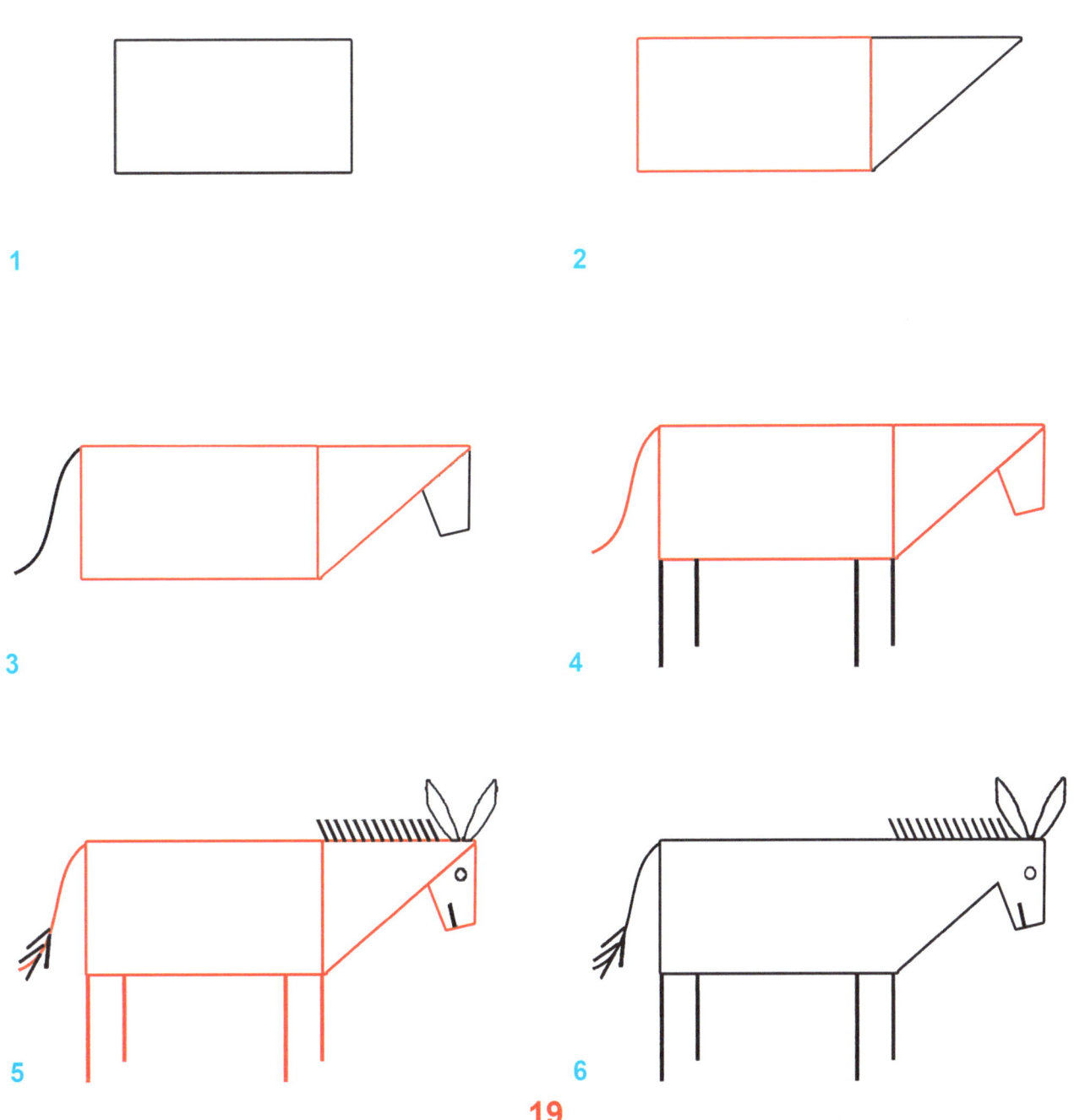

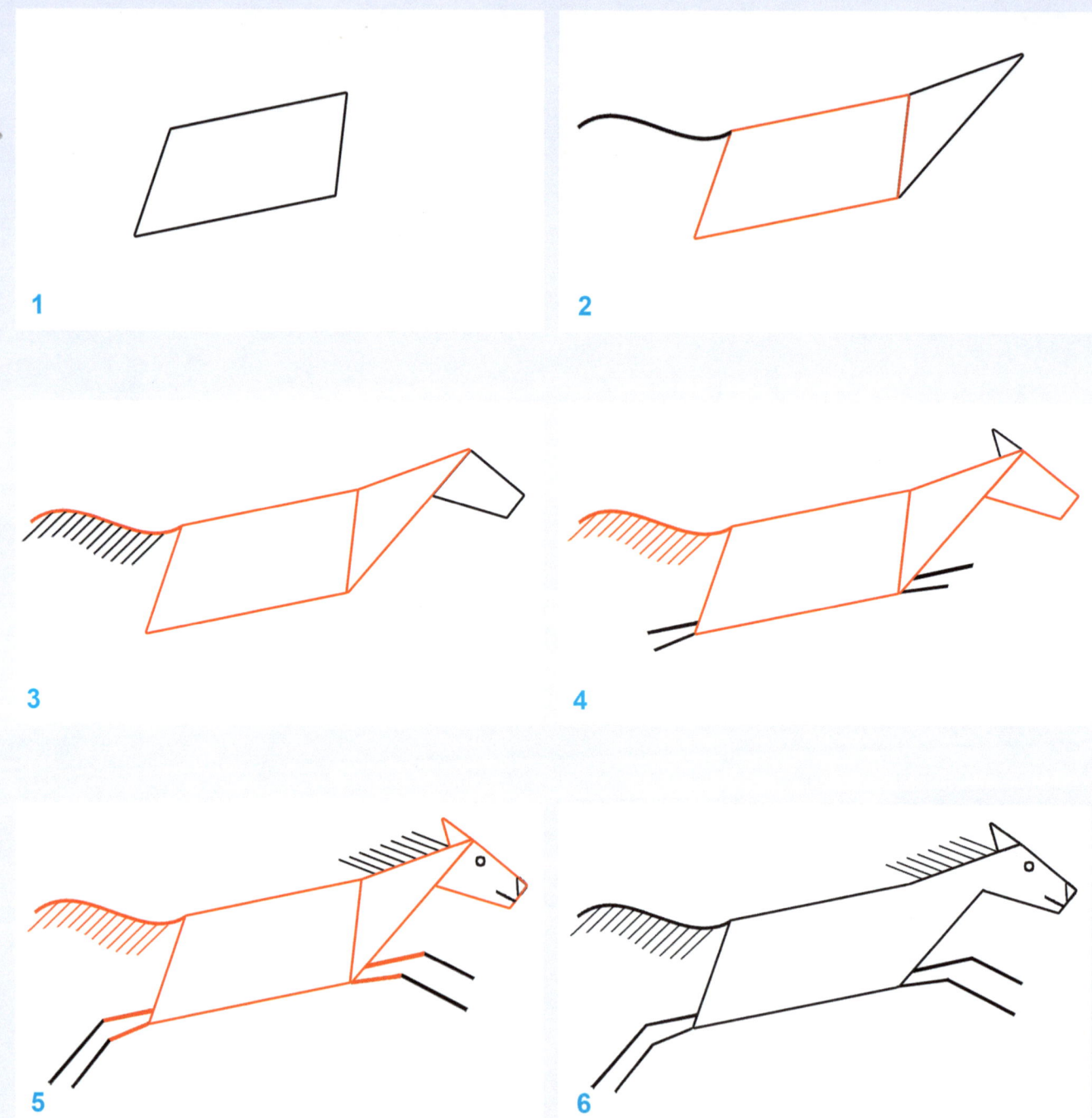

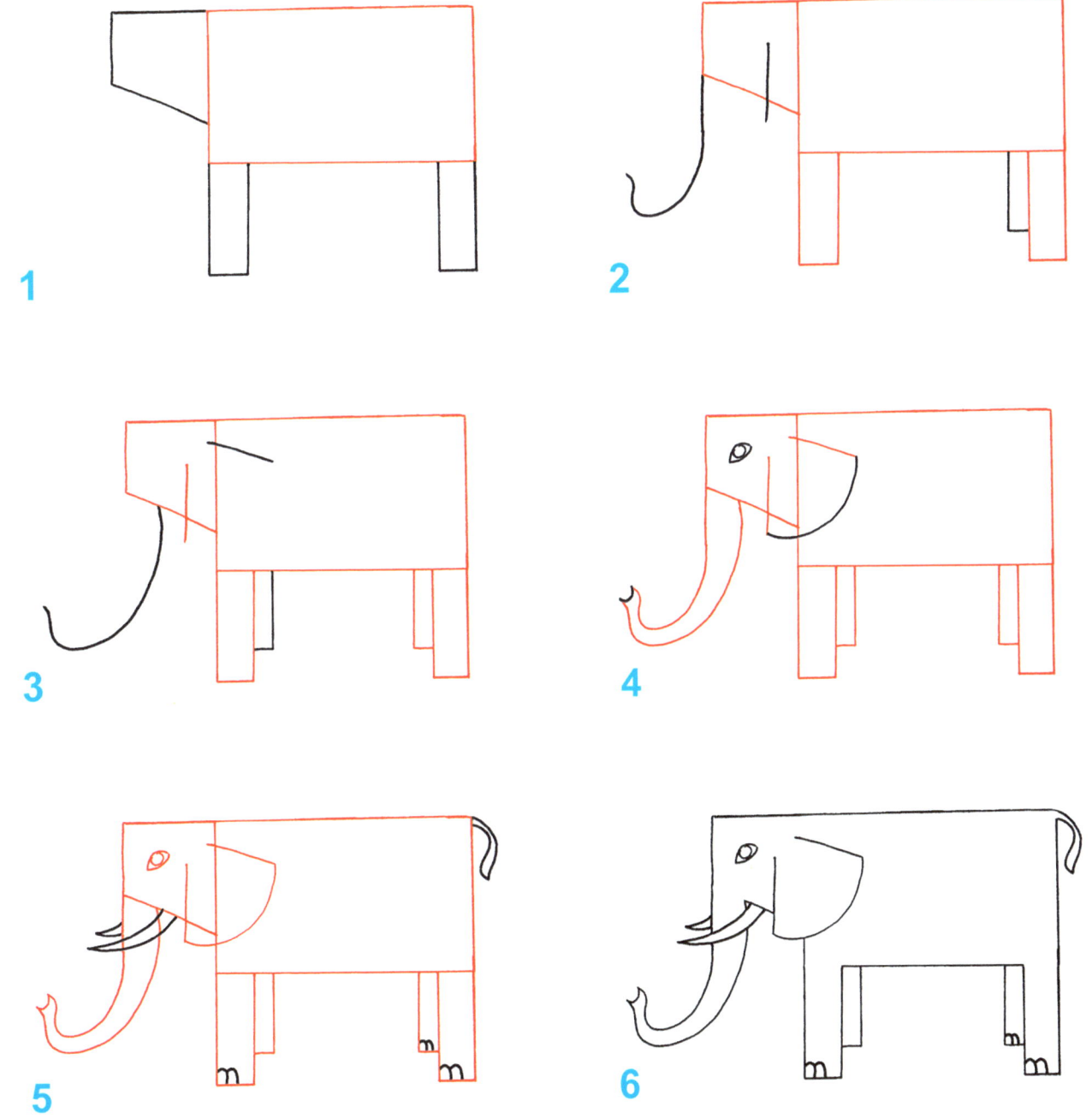

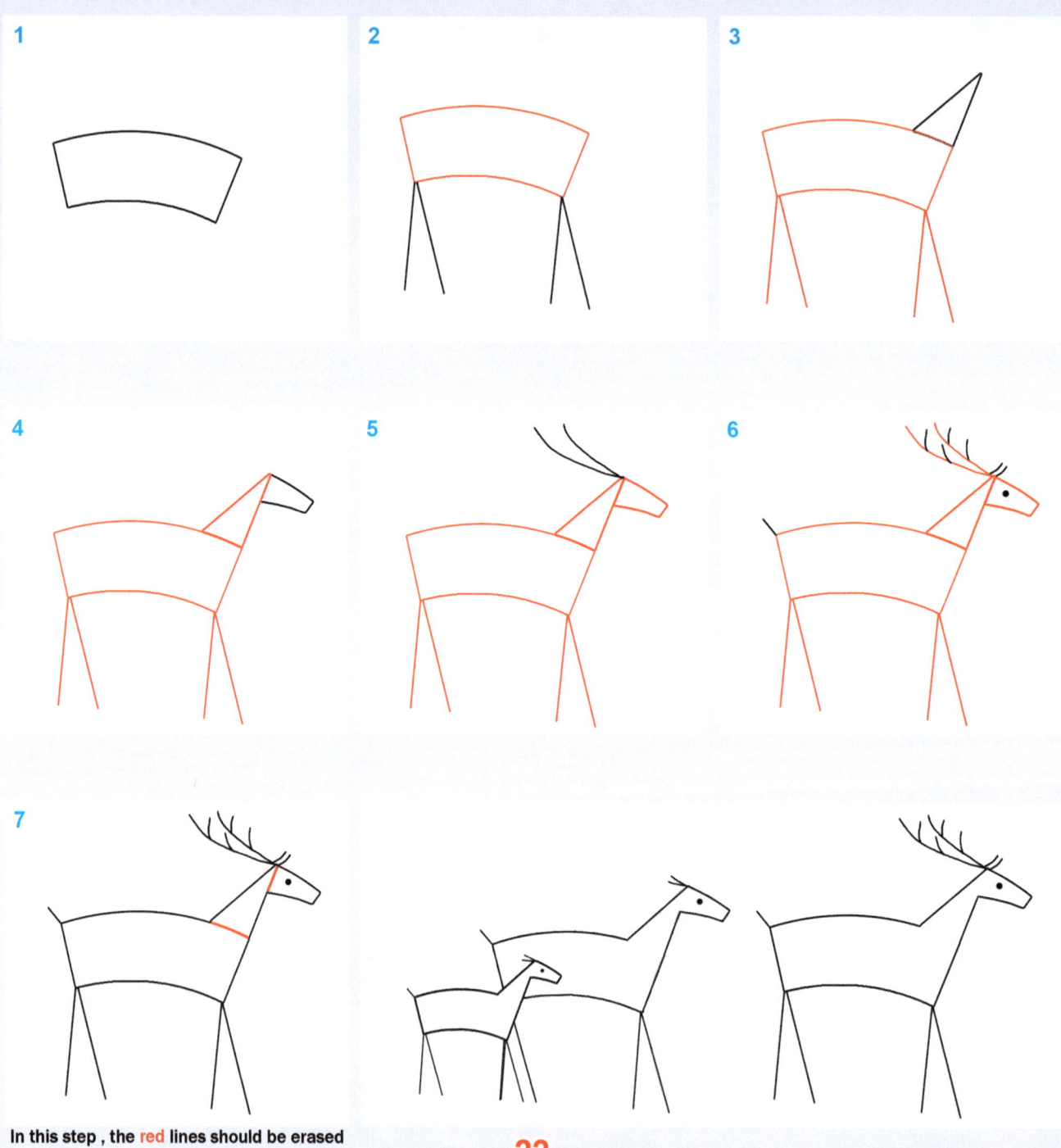

1

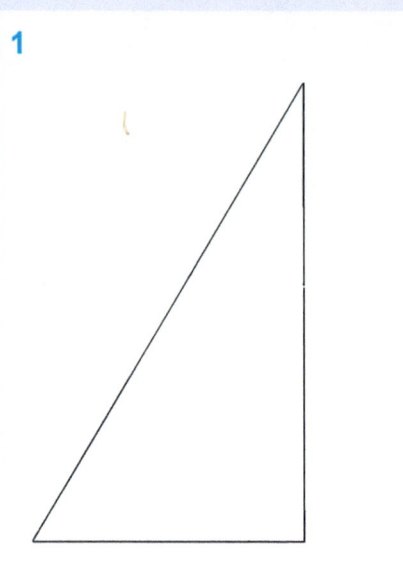

2

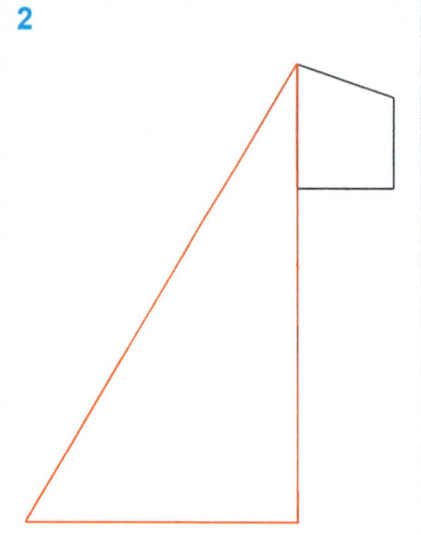

3

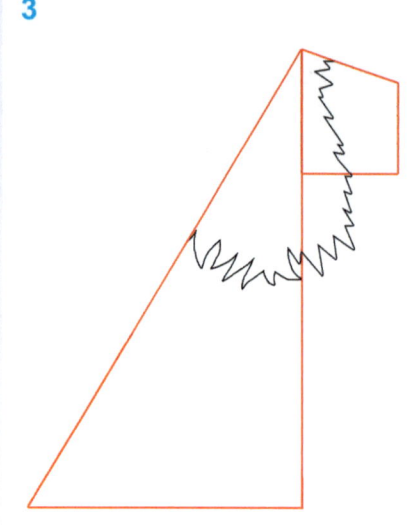

4

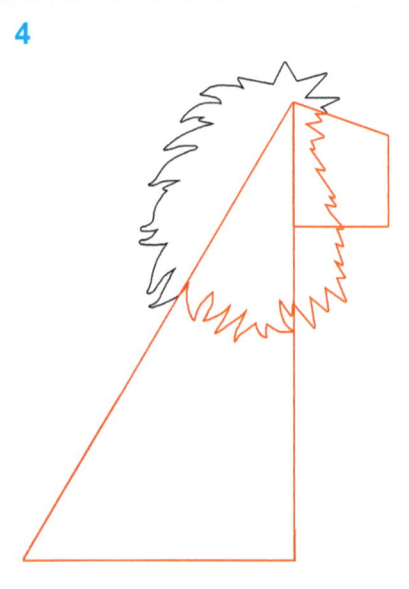

5

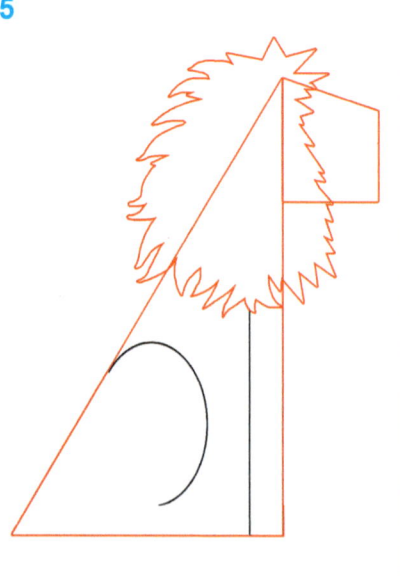

6

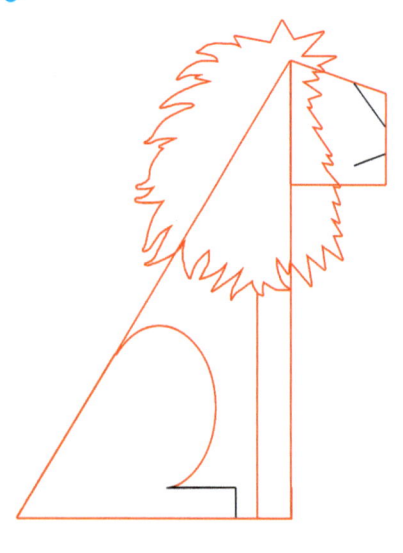

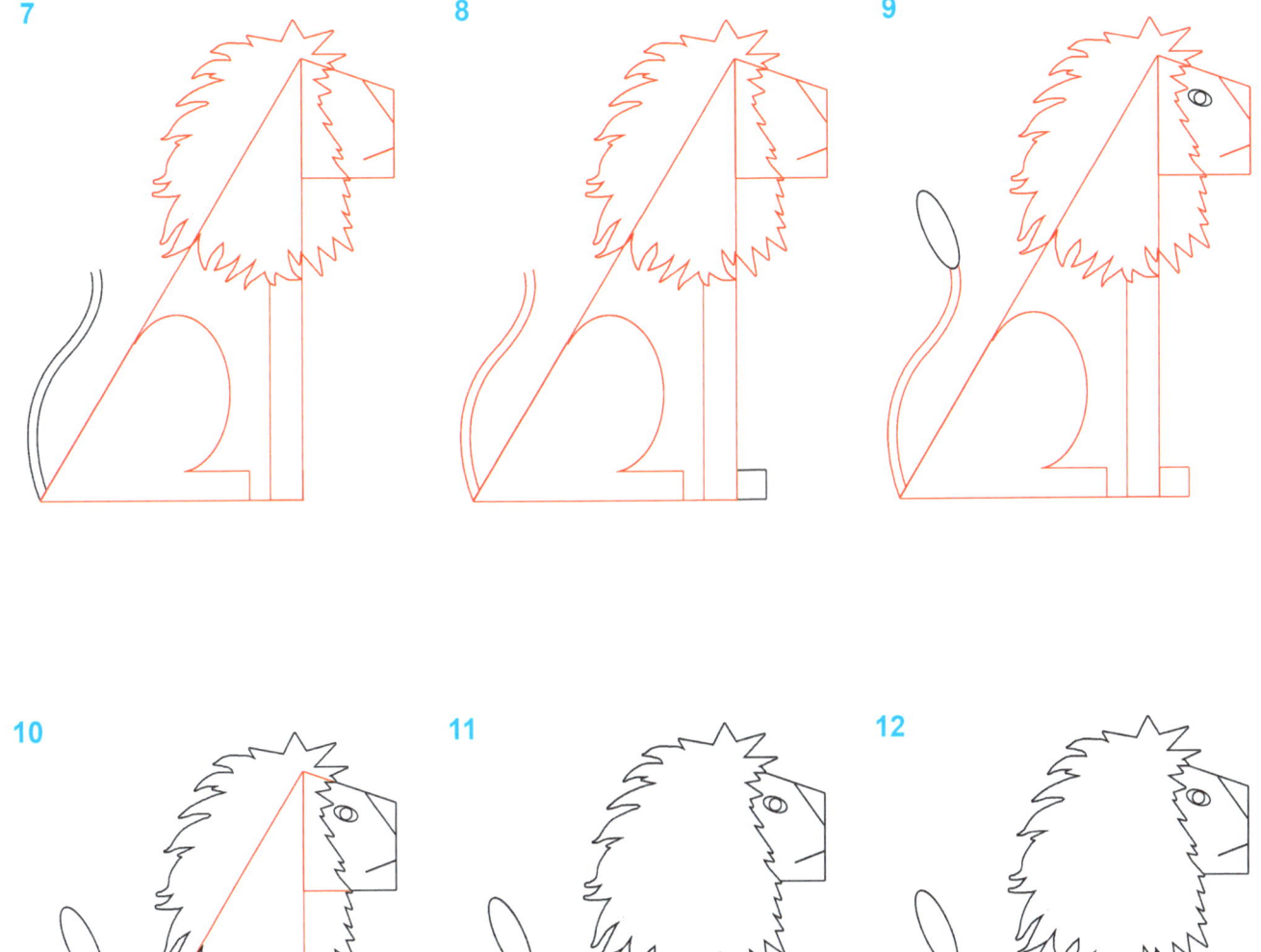

In this step , the red lines should be erased

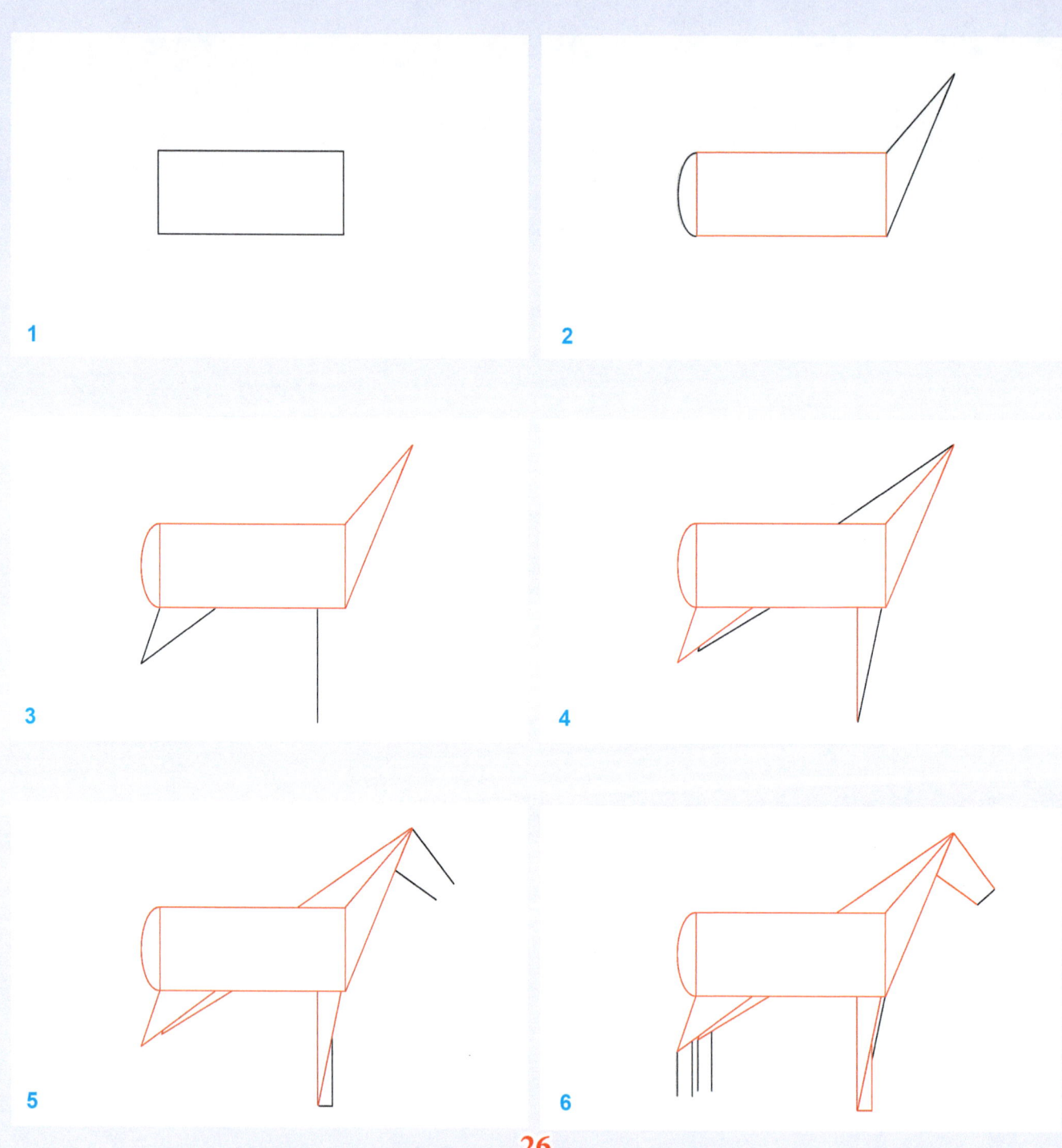

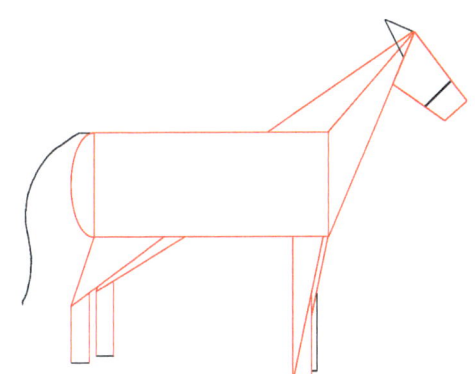

7

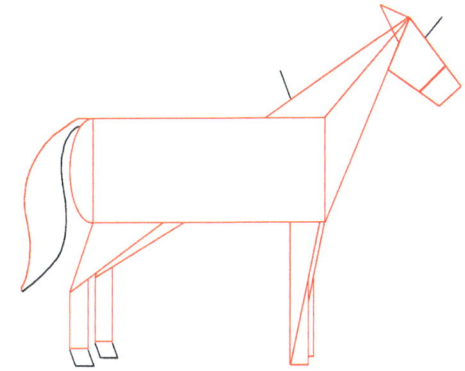

8

10

9

11

12

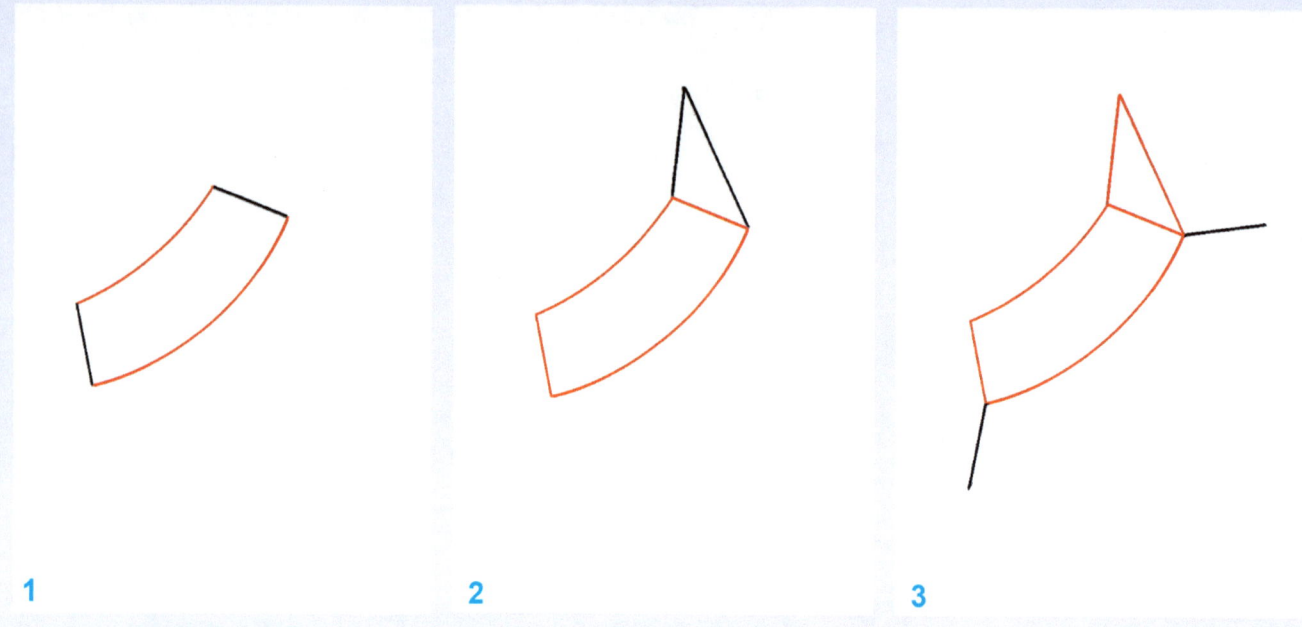
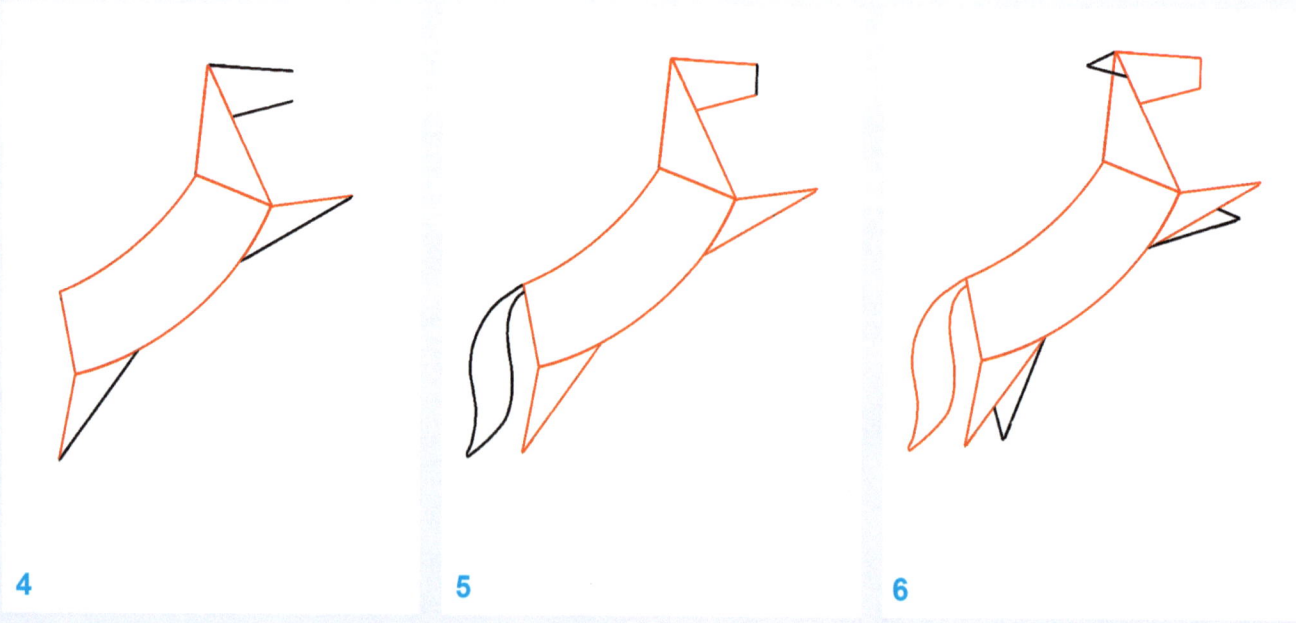

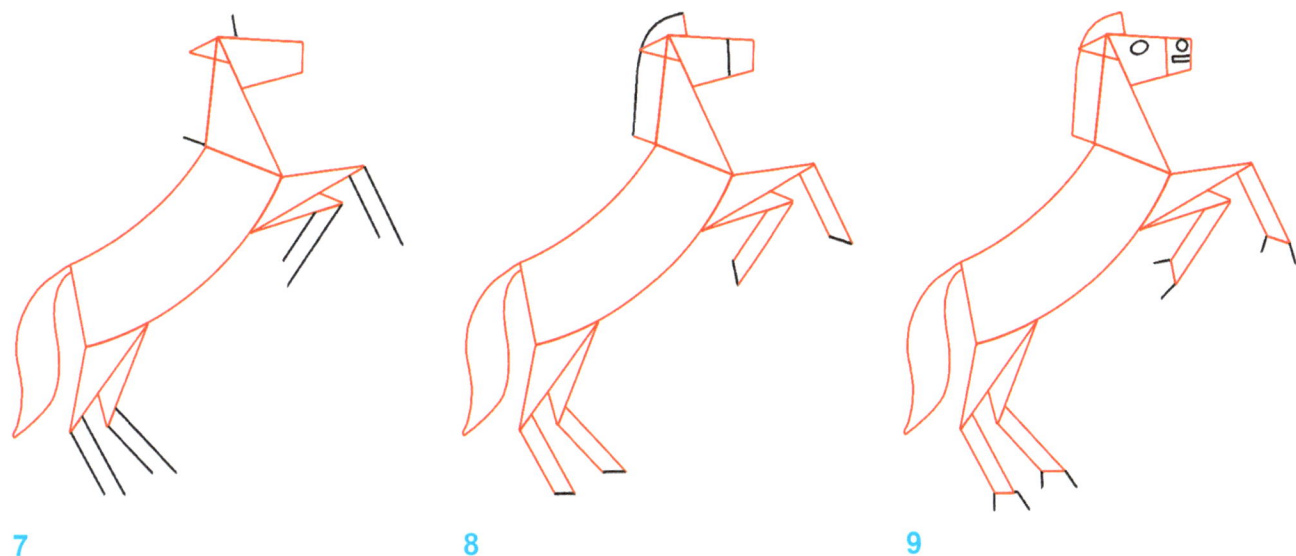
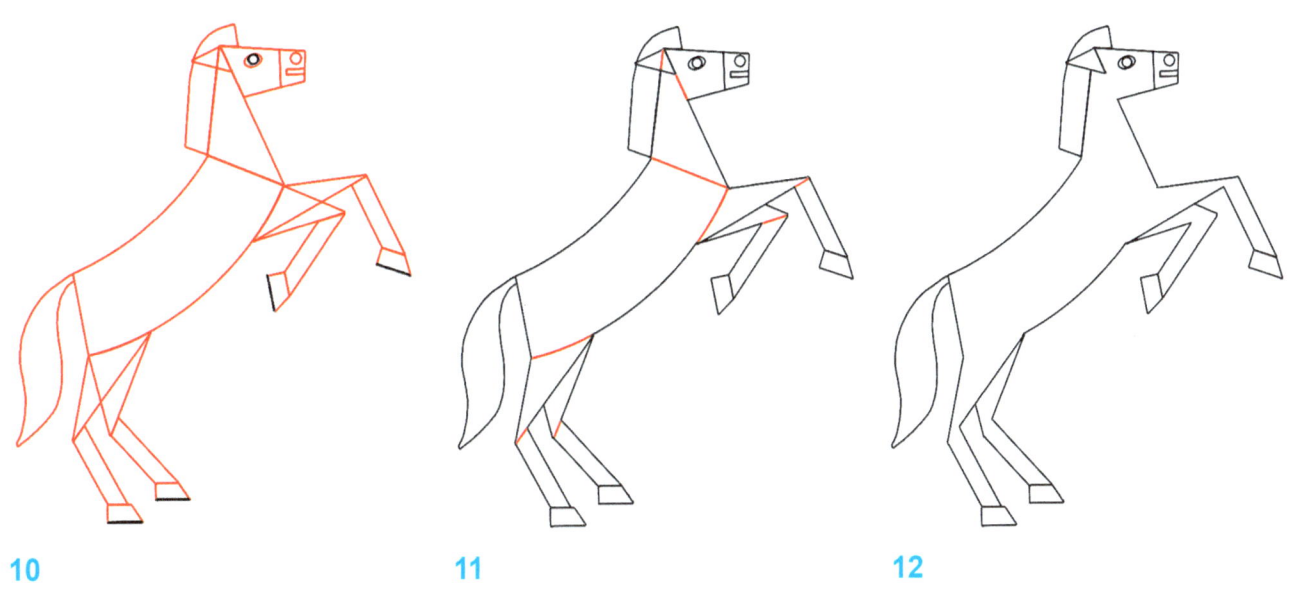

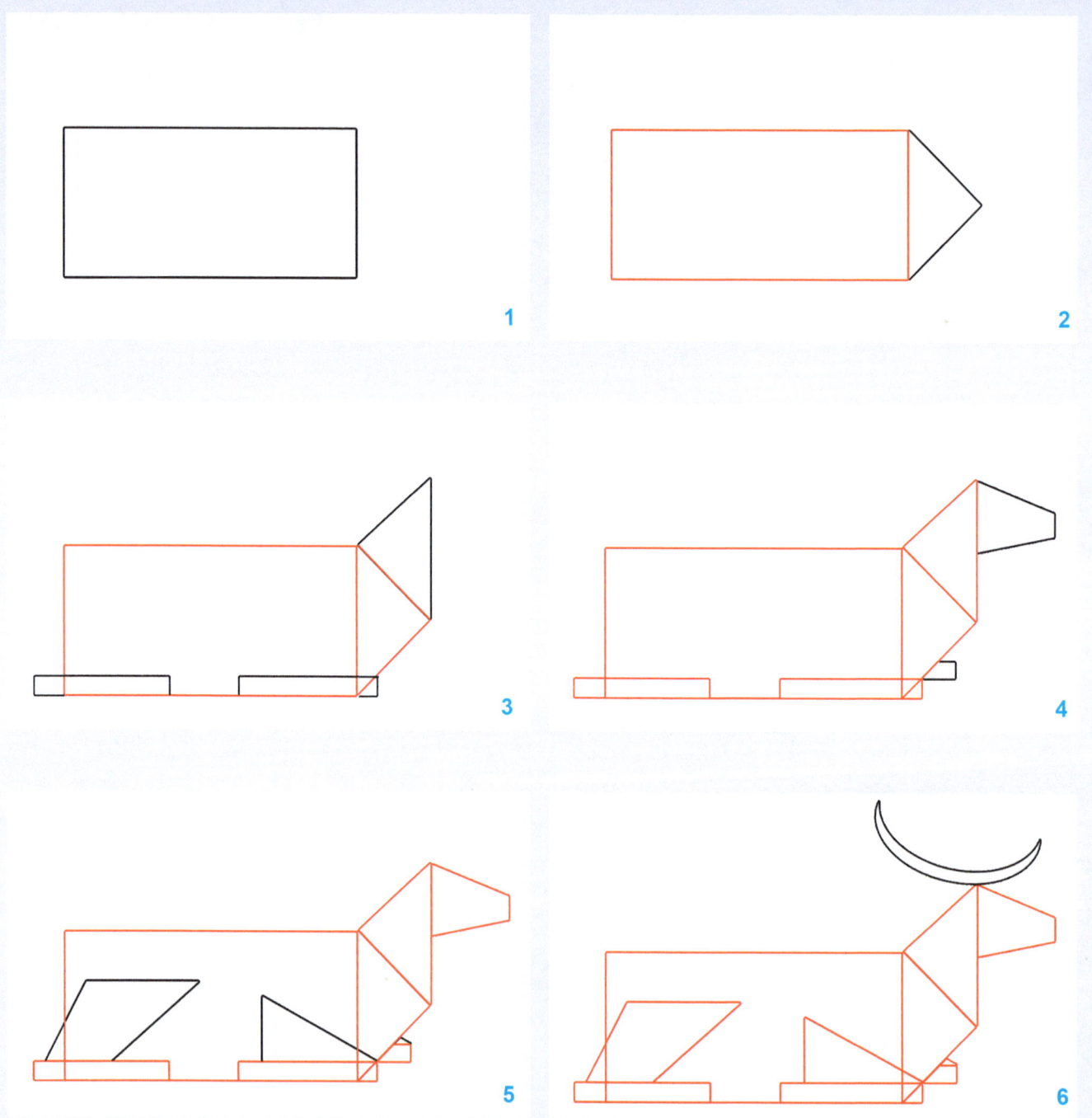

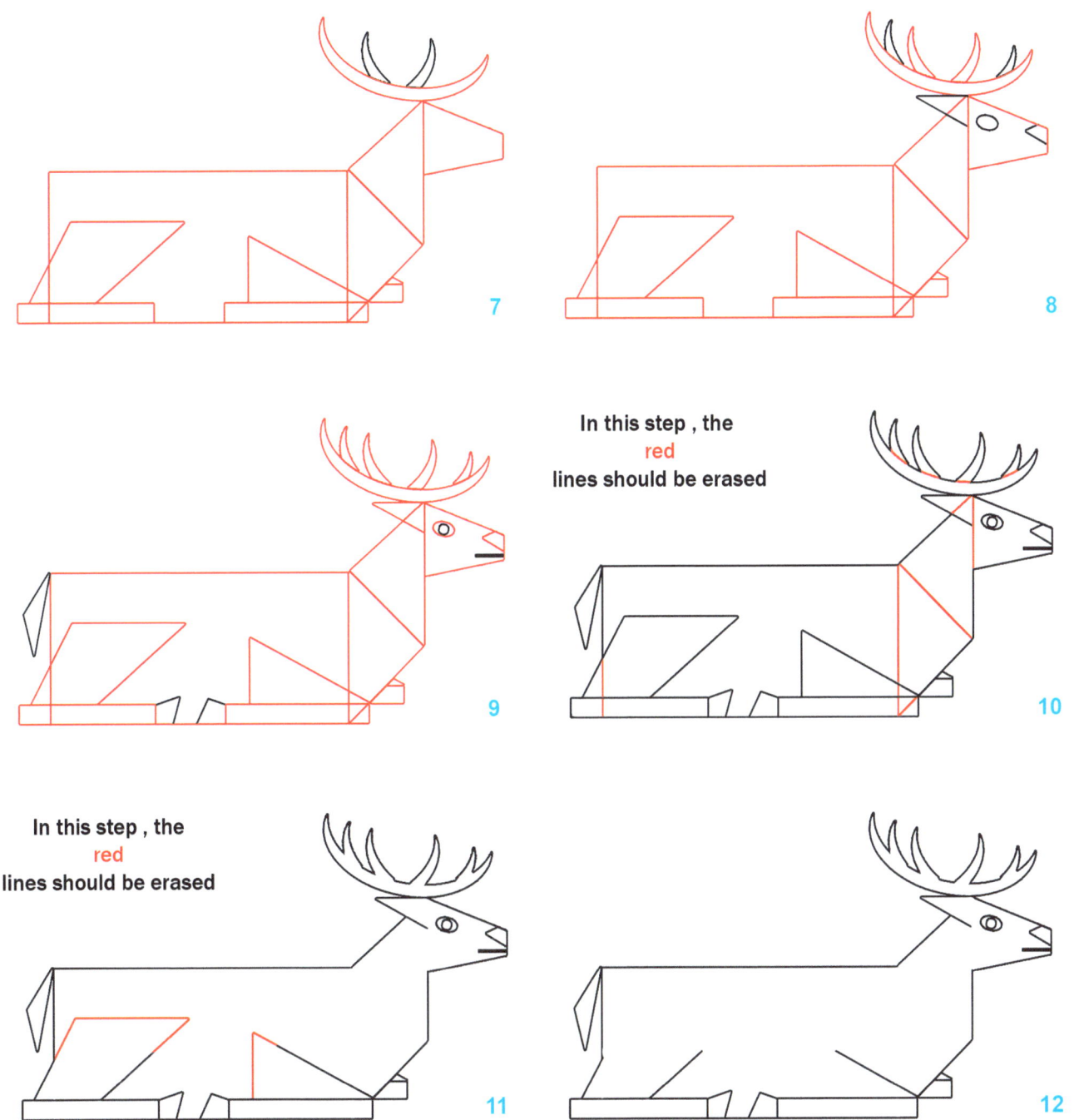

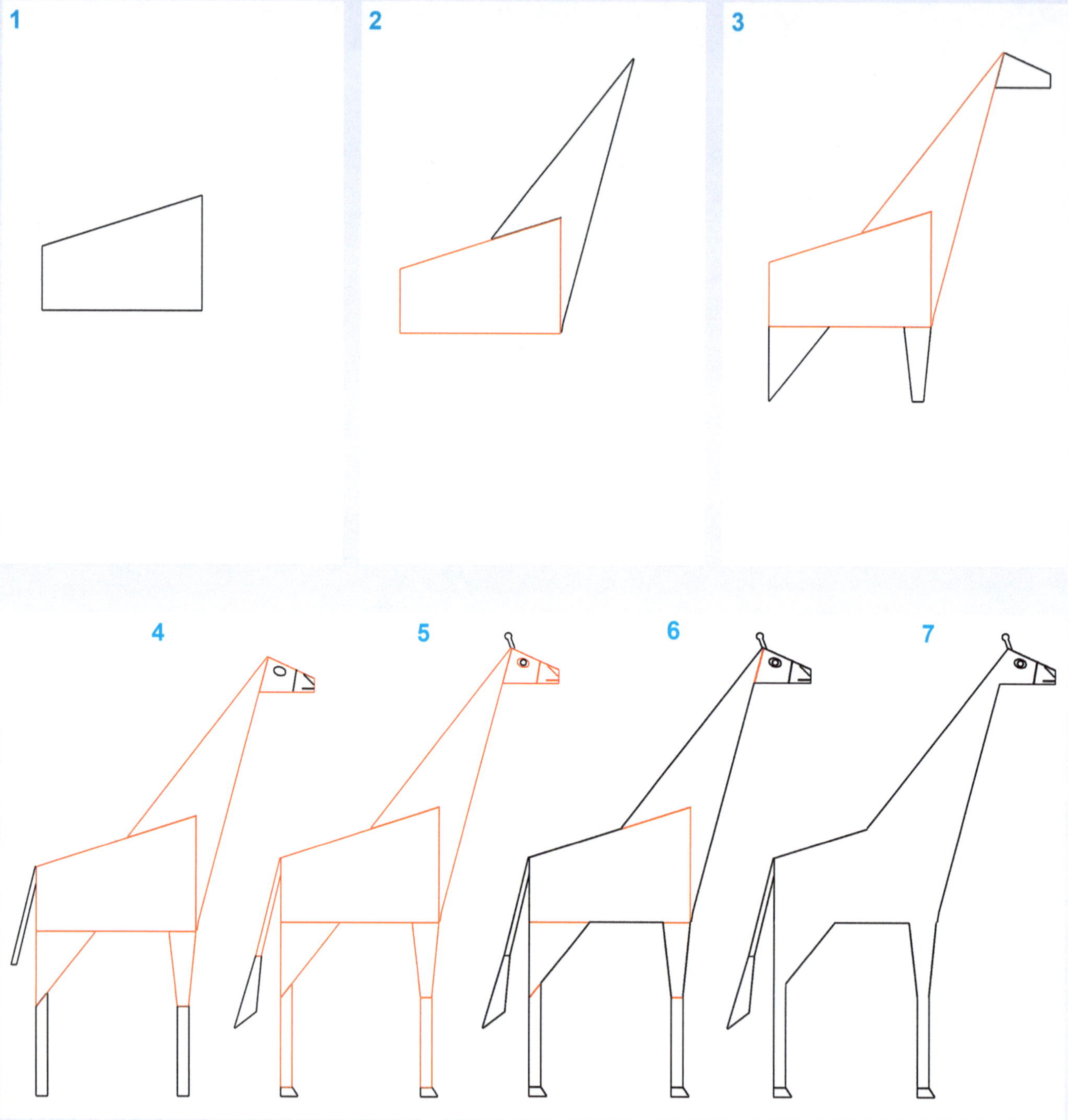

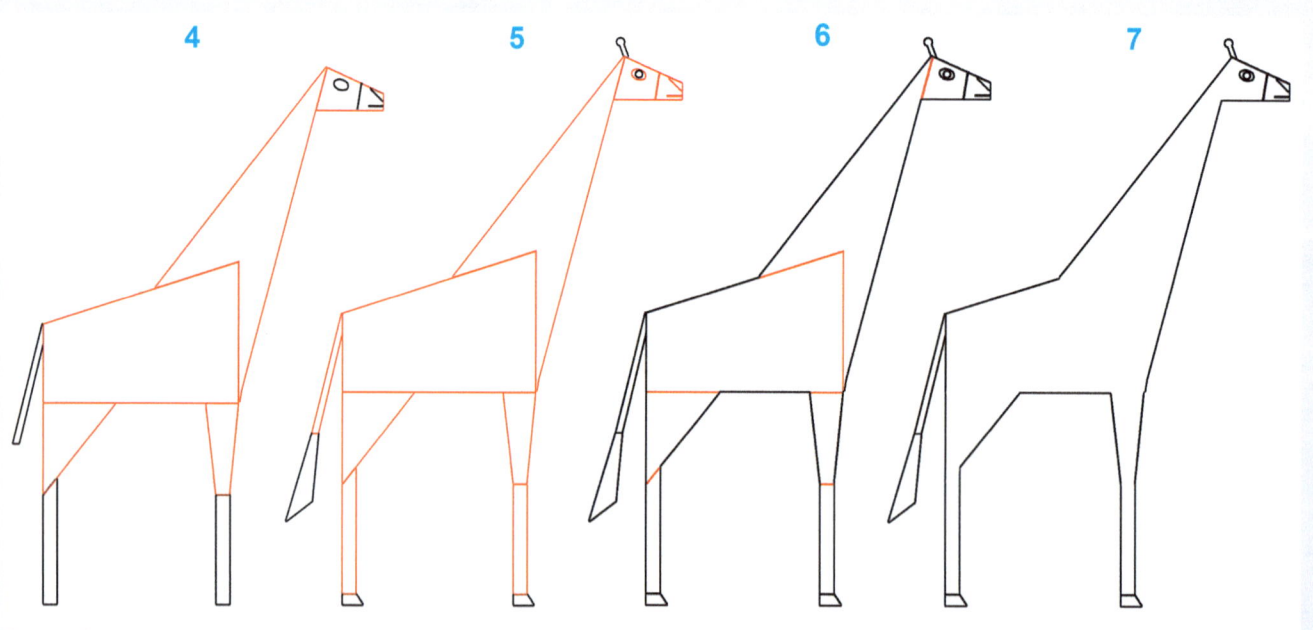

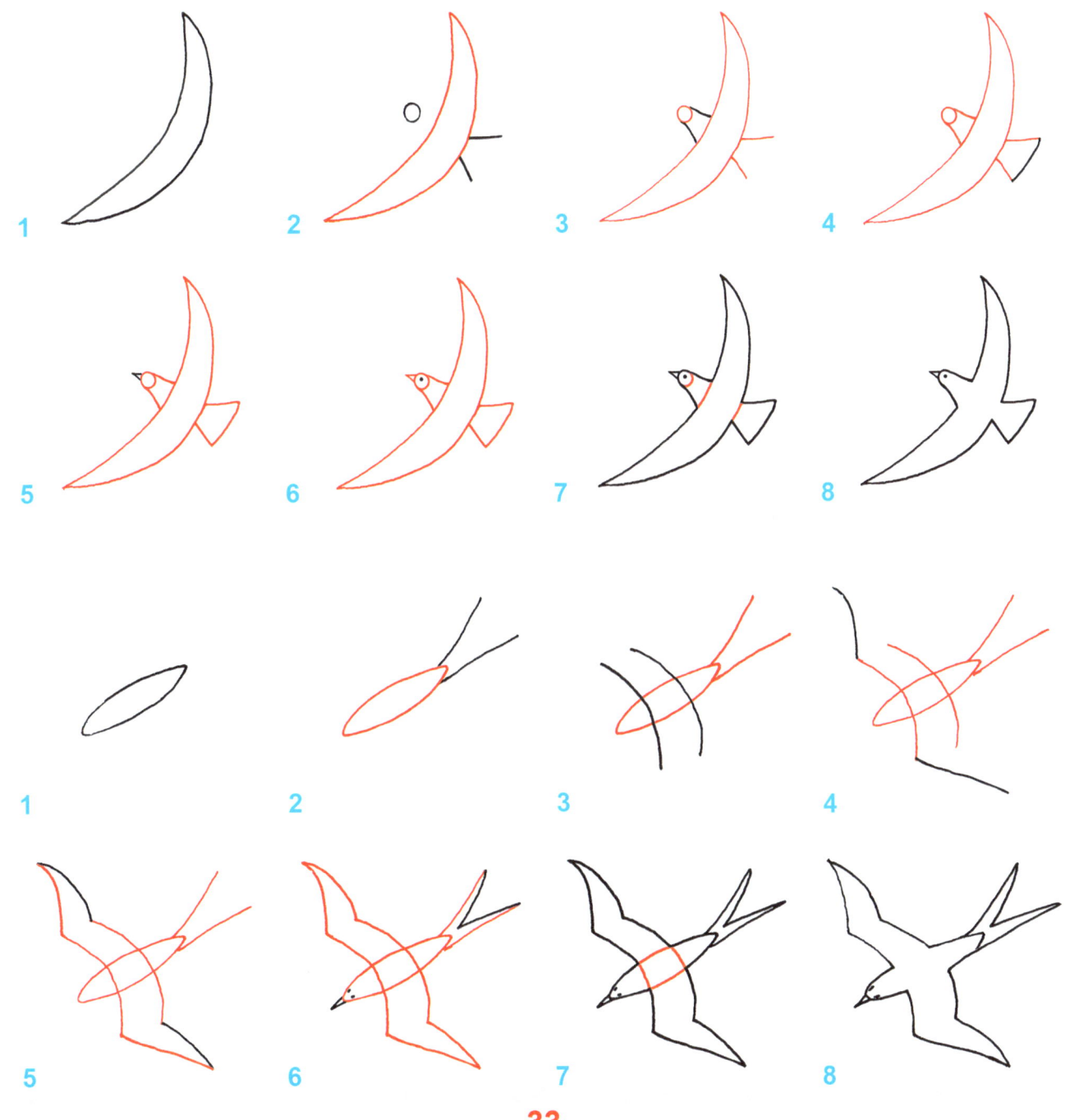

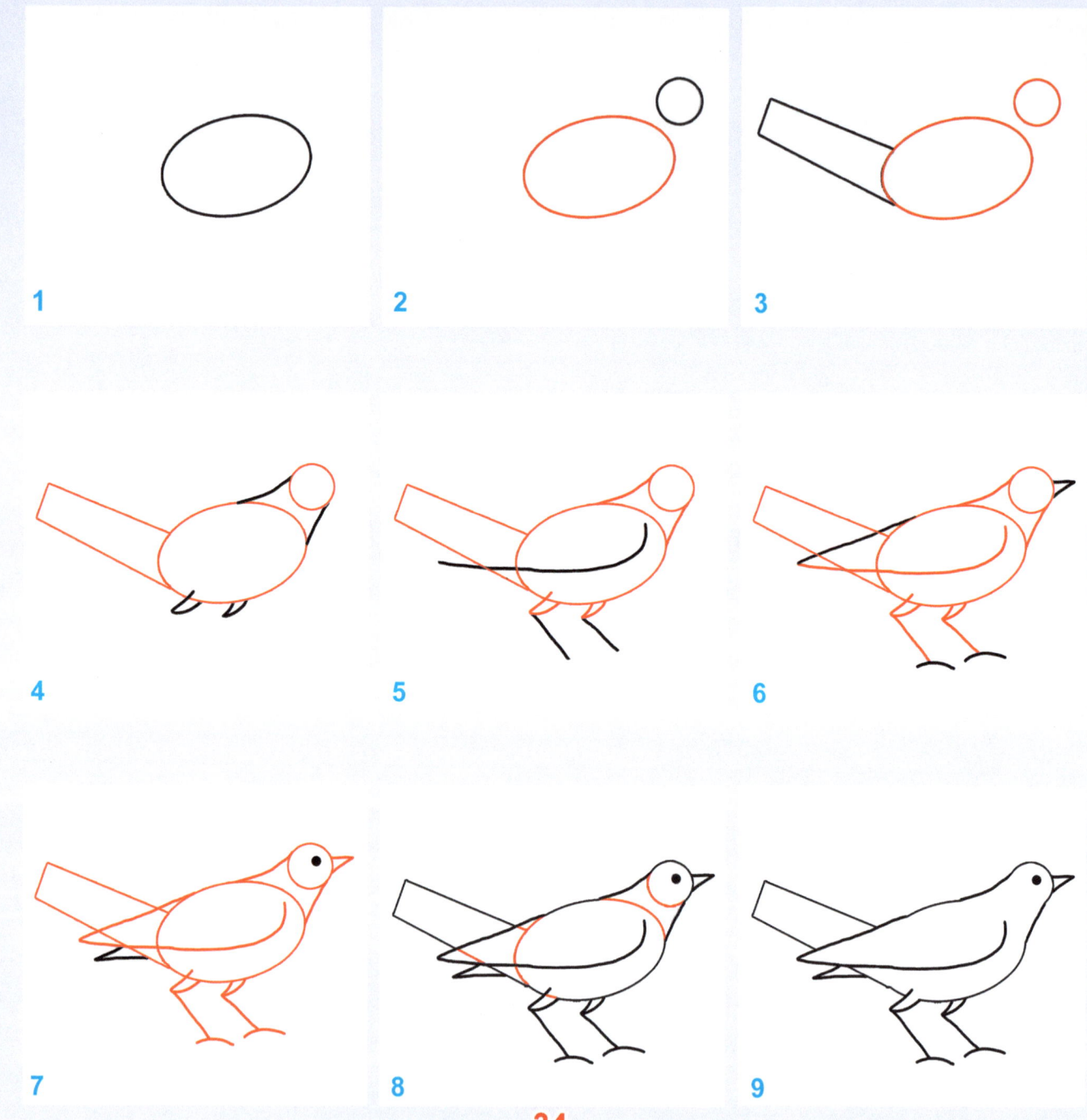

1
2
3
4
5
6
7
8
9

35

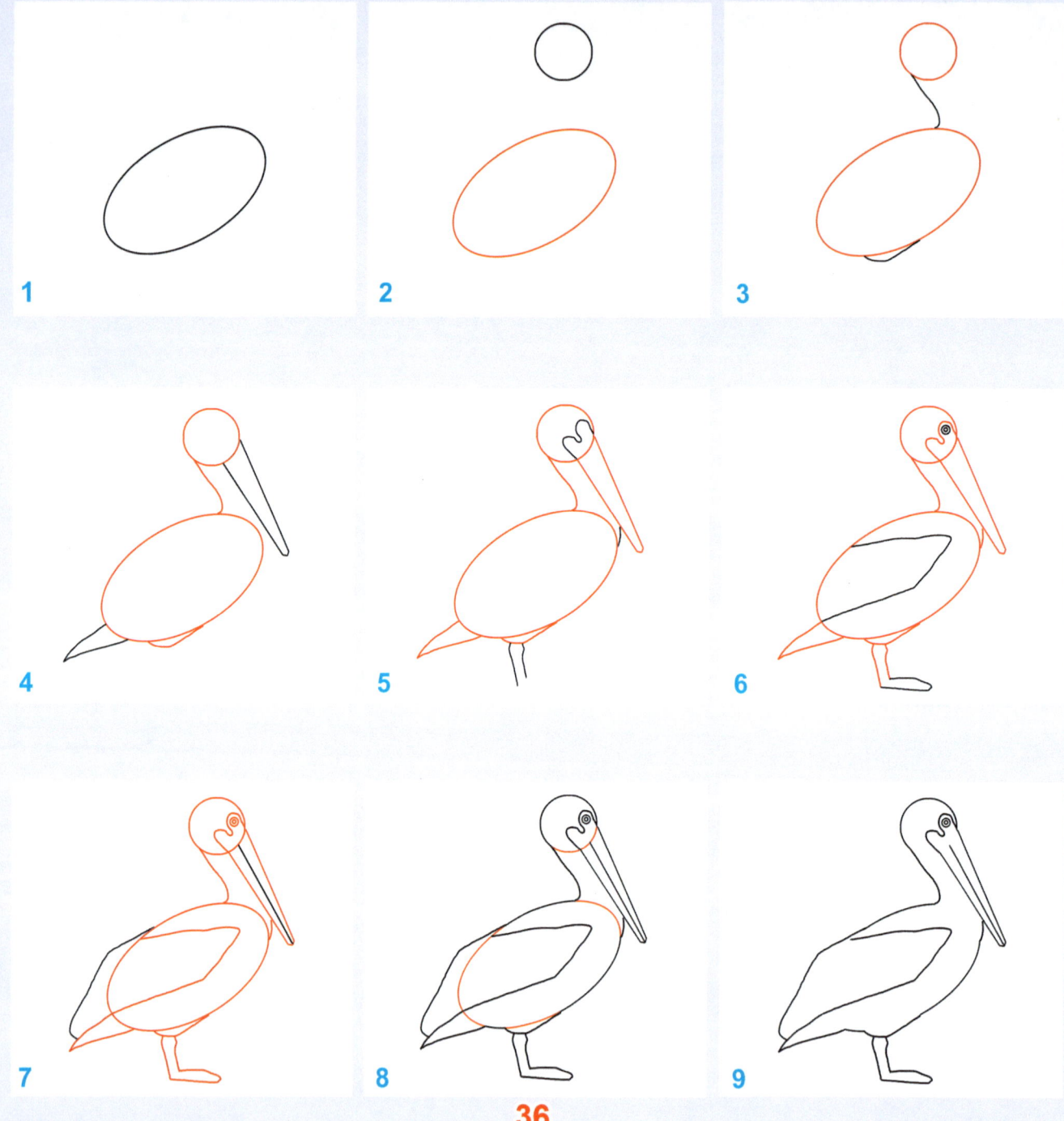

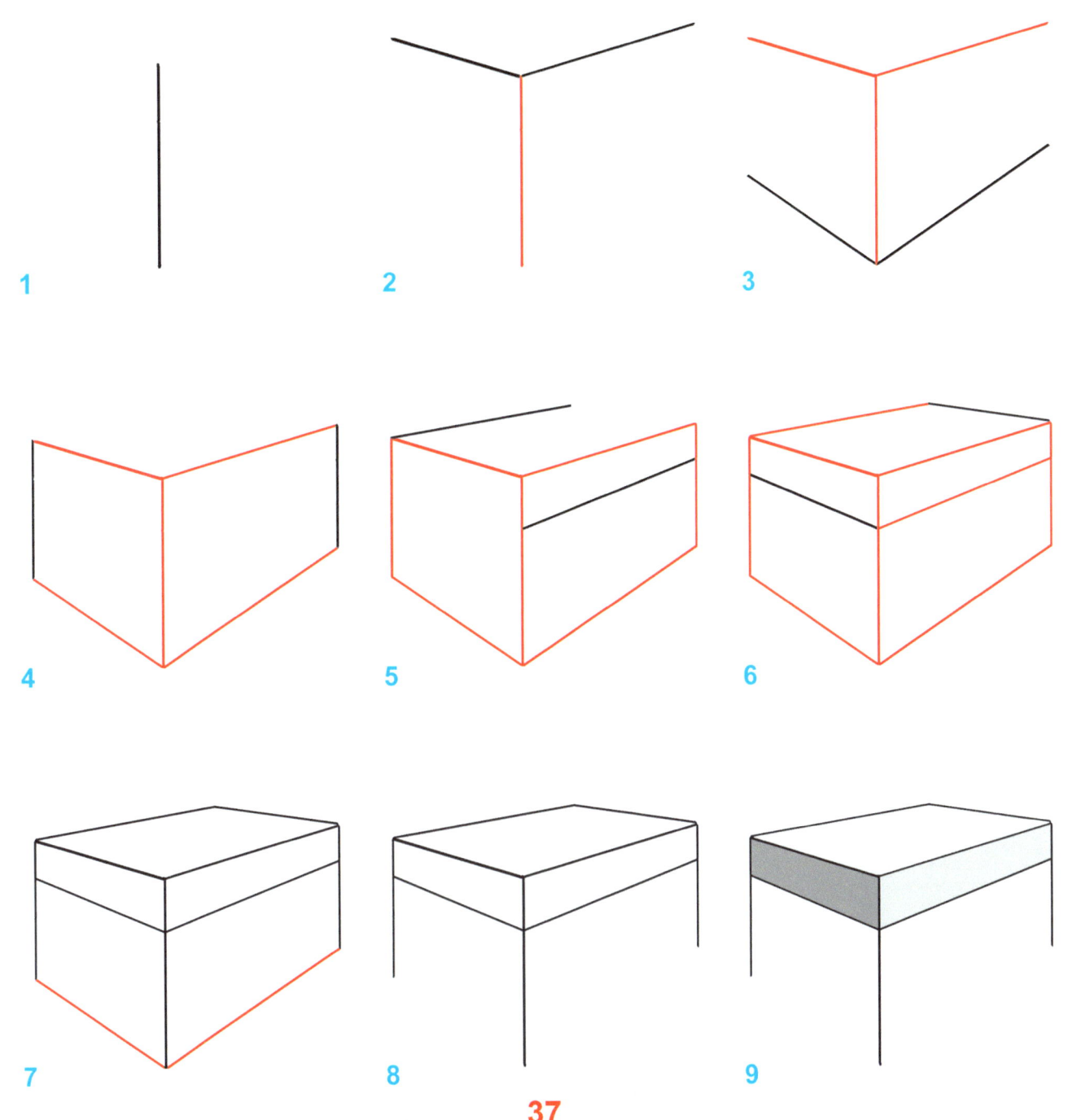

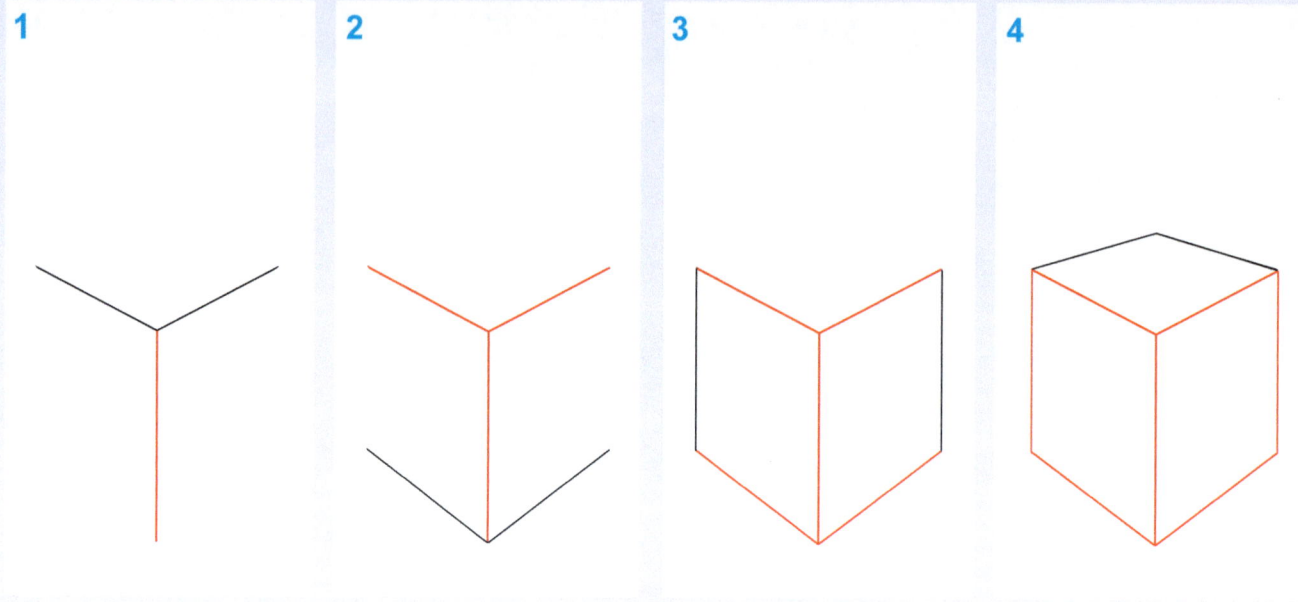
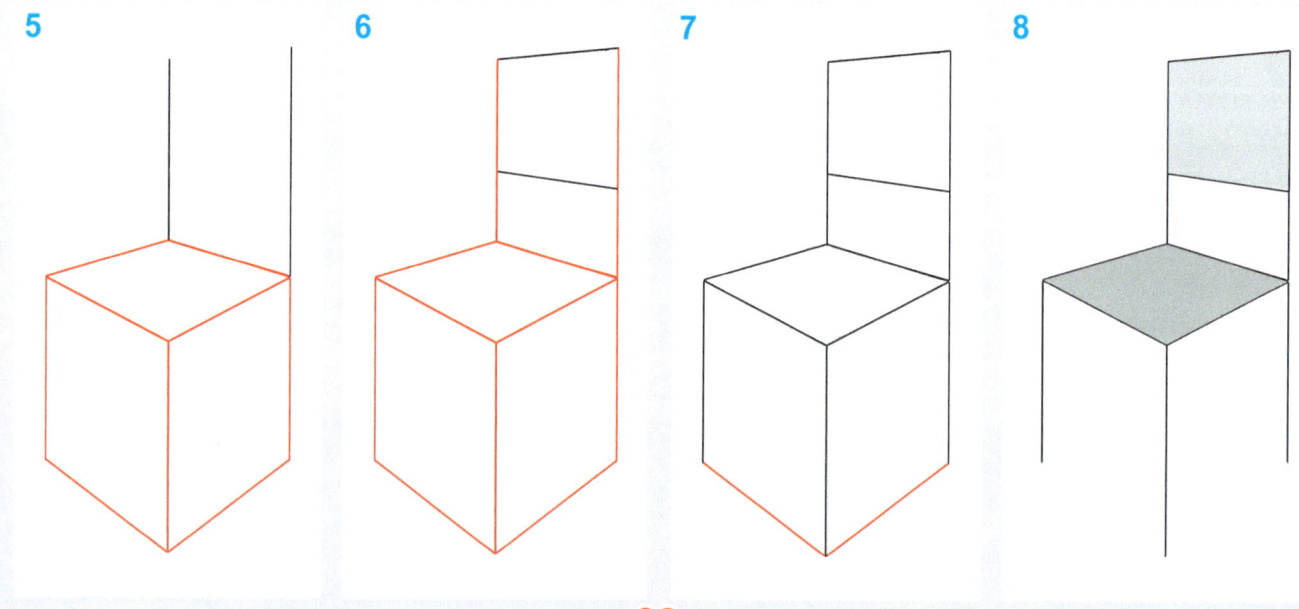

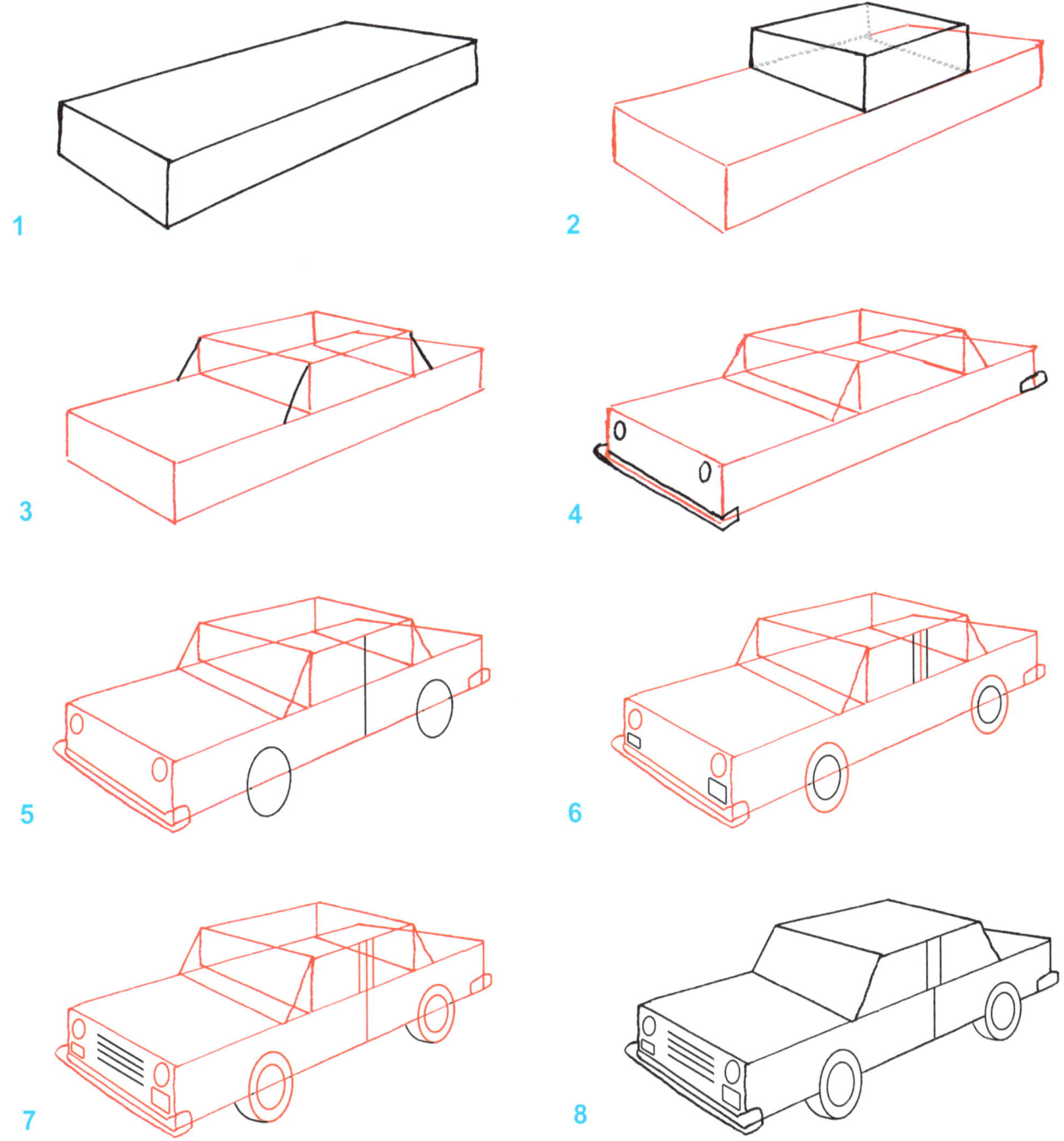

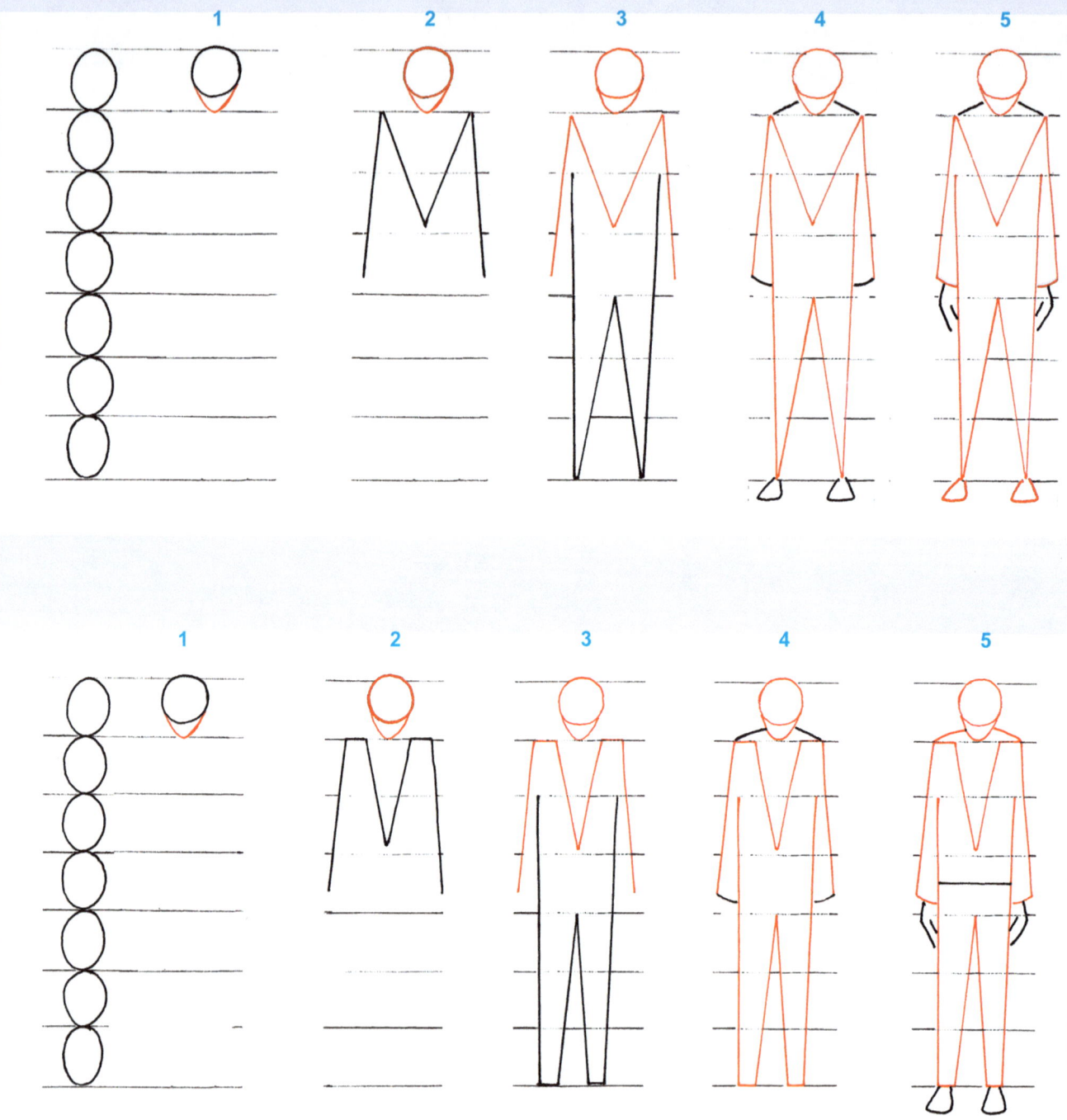

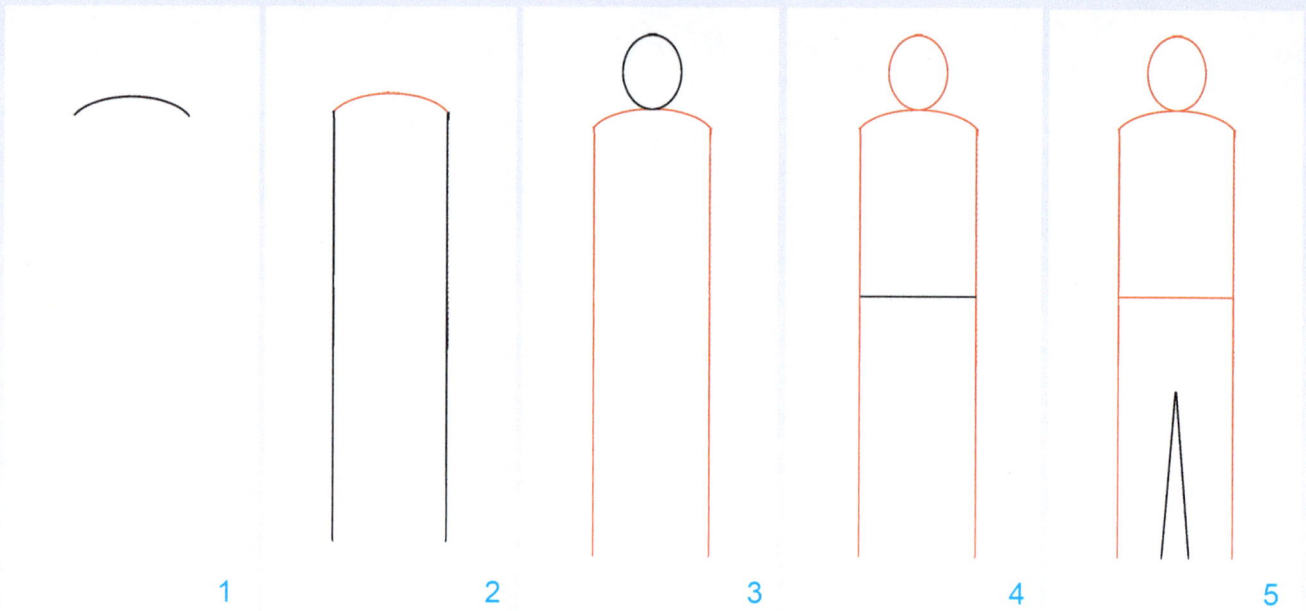
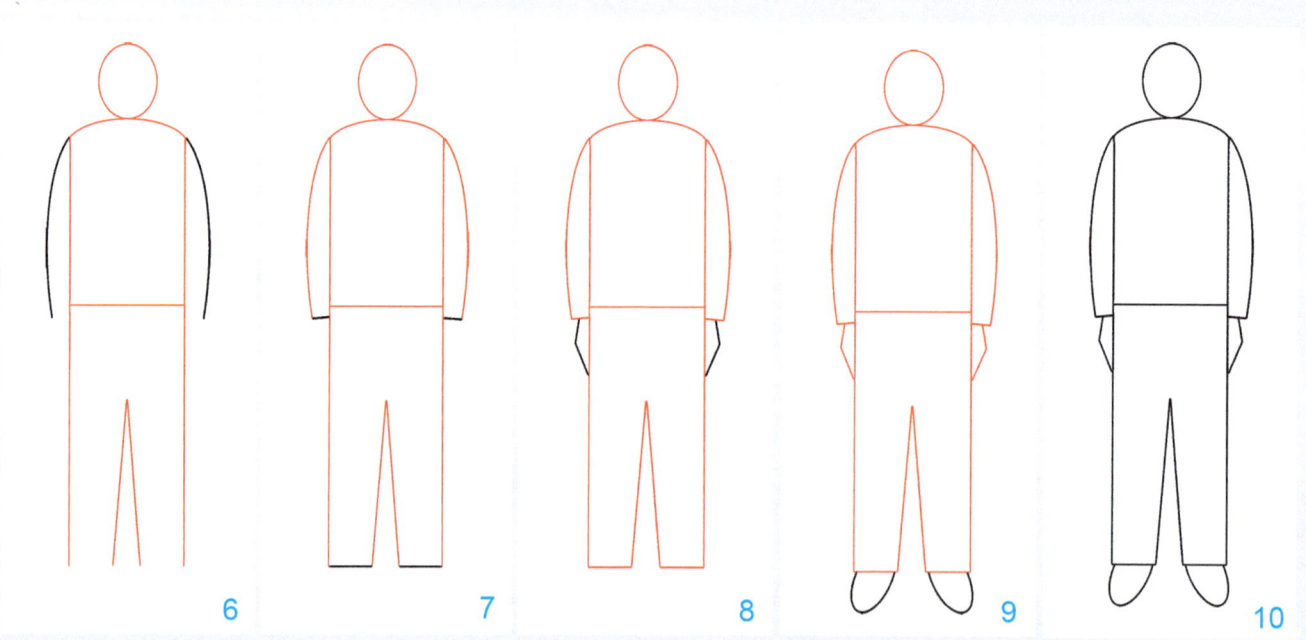

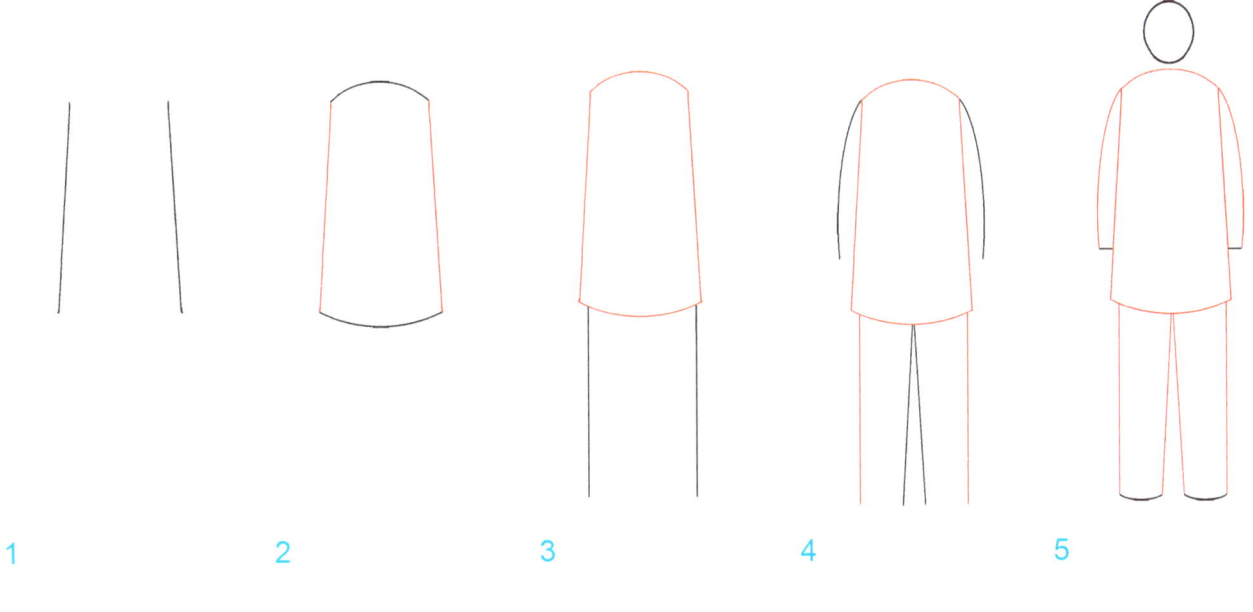

1 2 3 4 5

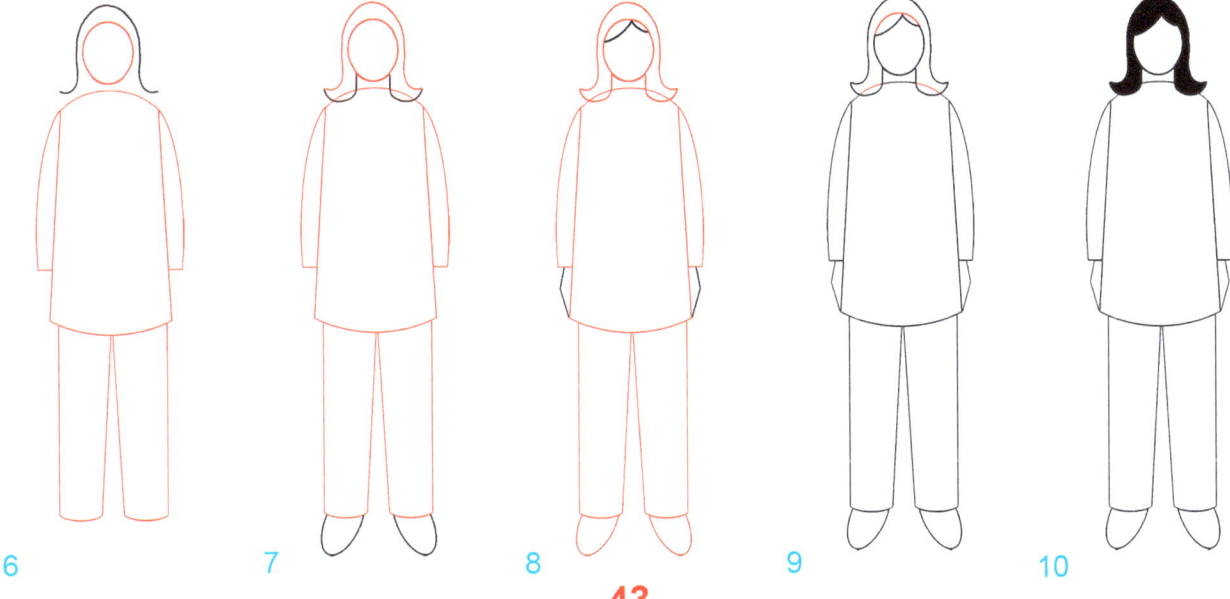

6 7 8 9 10

43

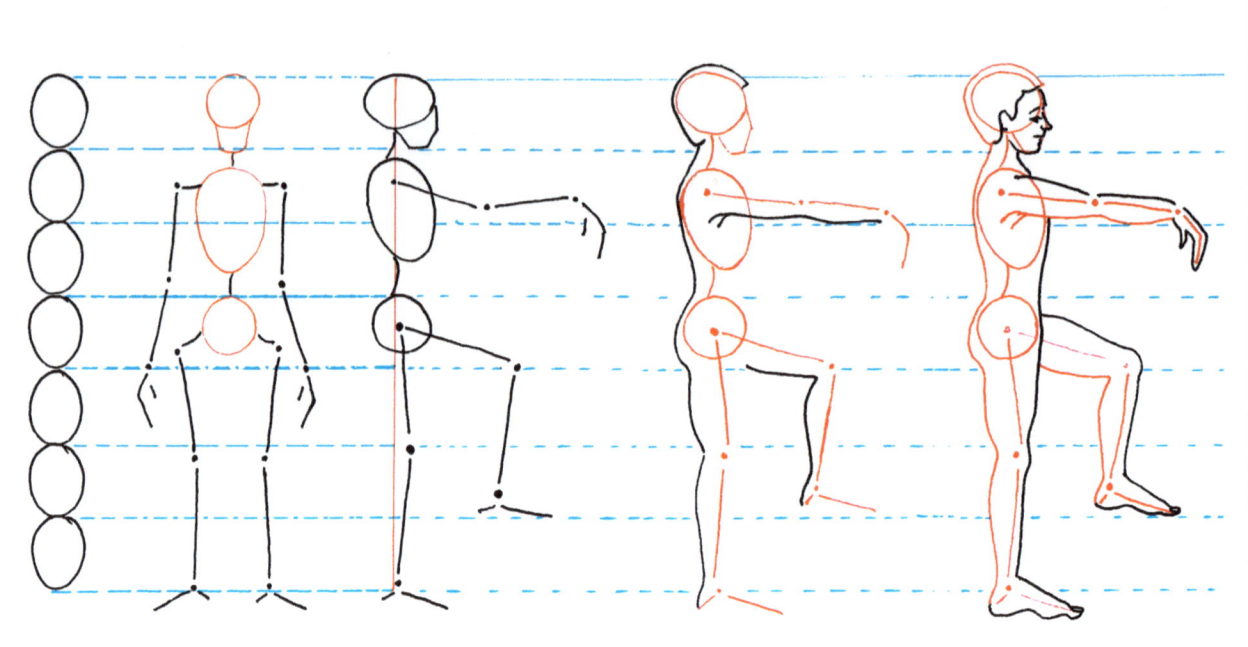
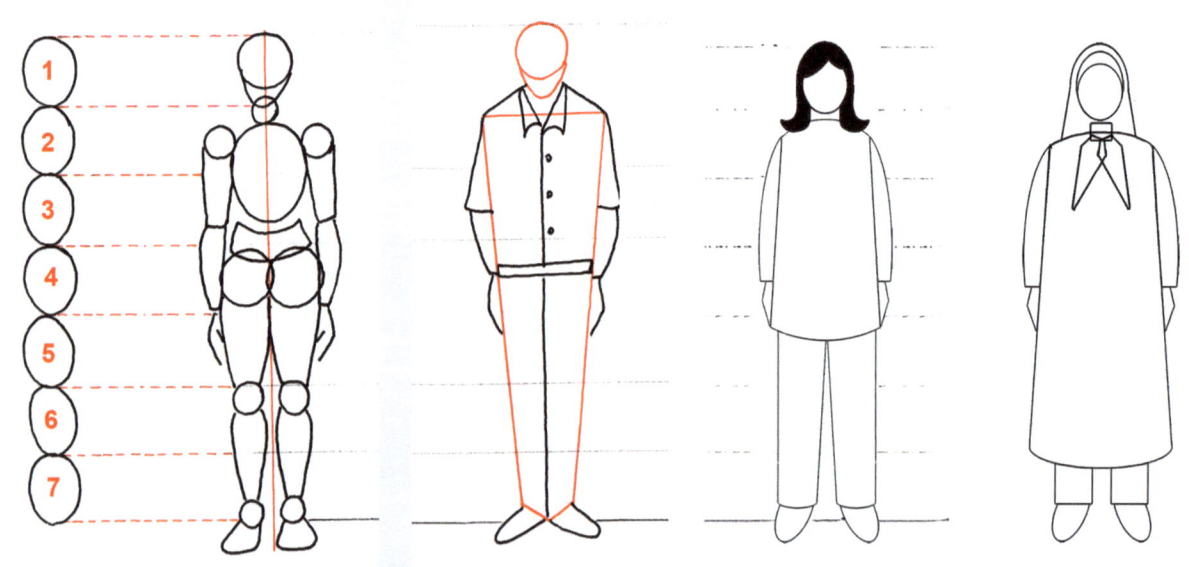

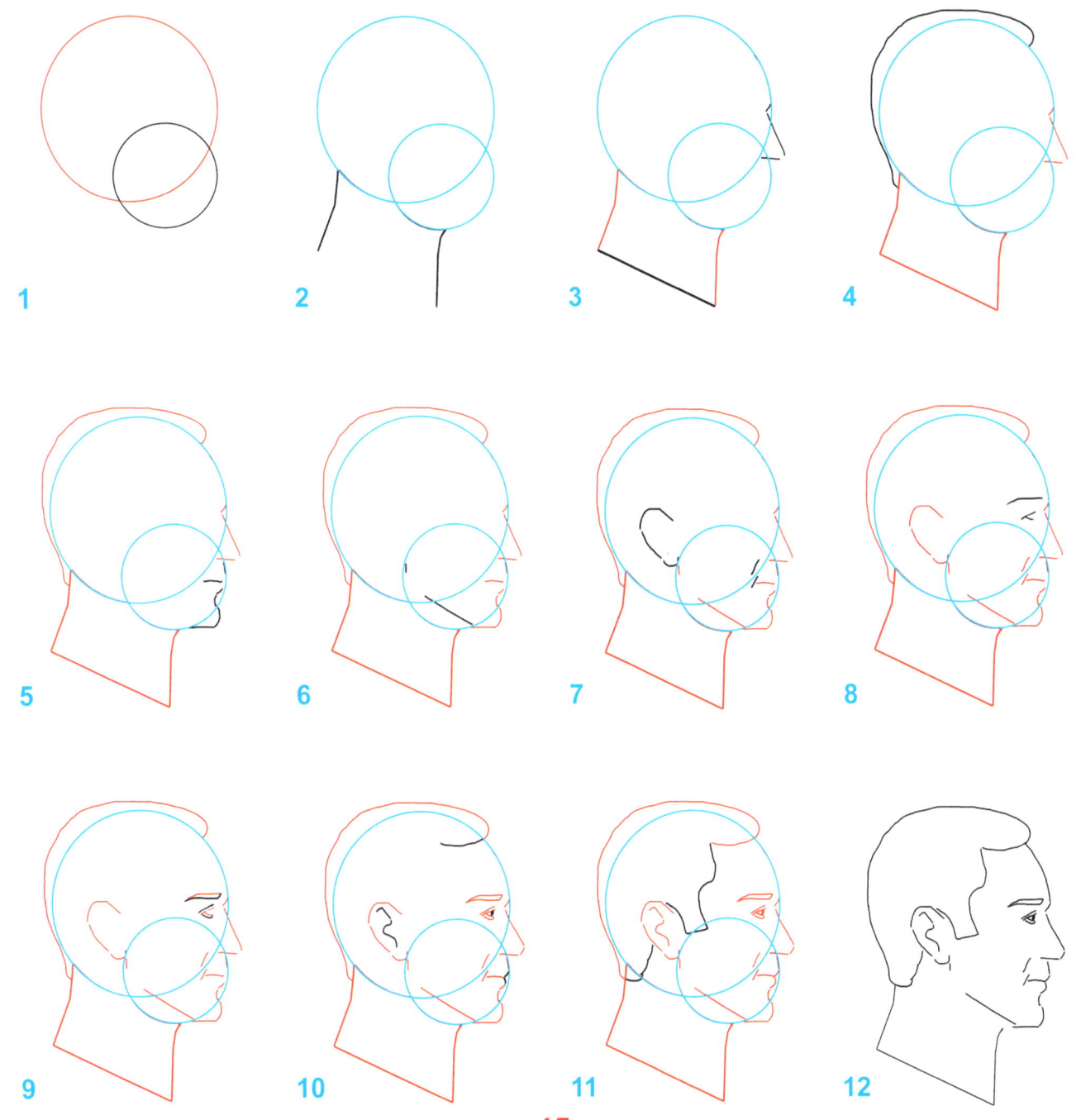

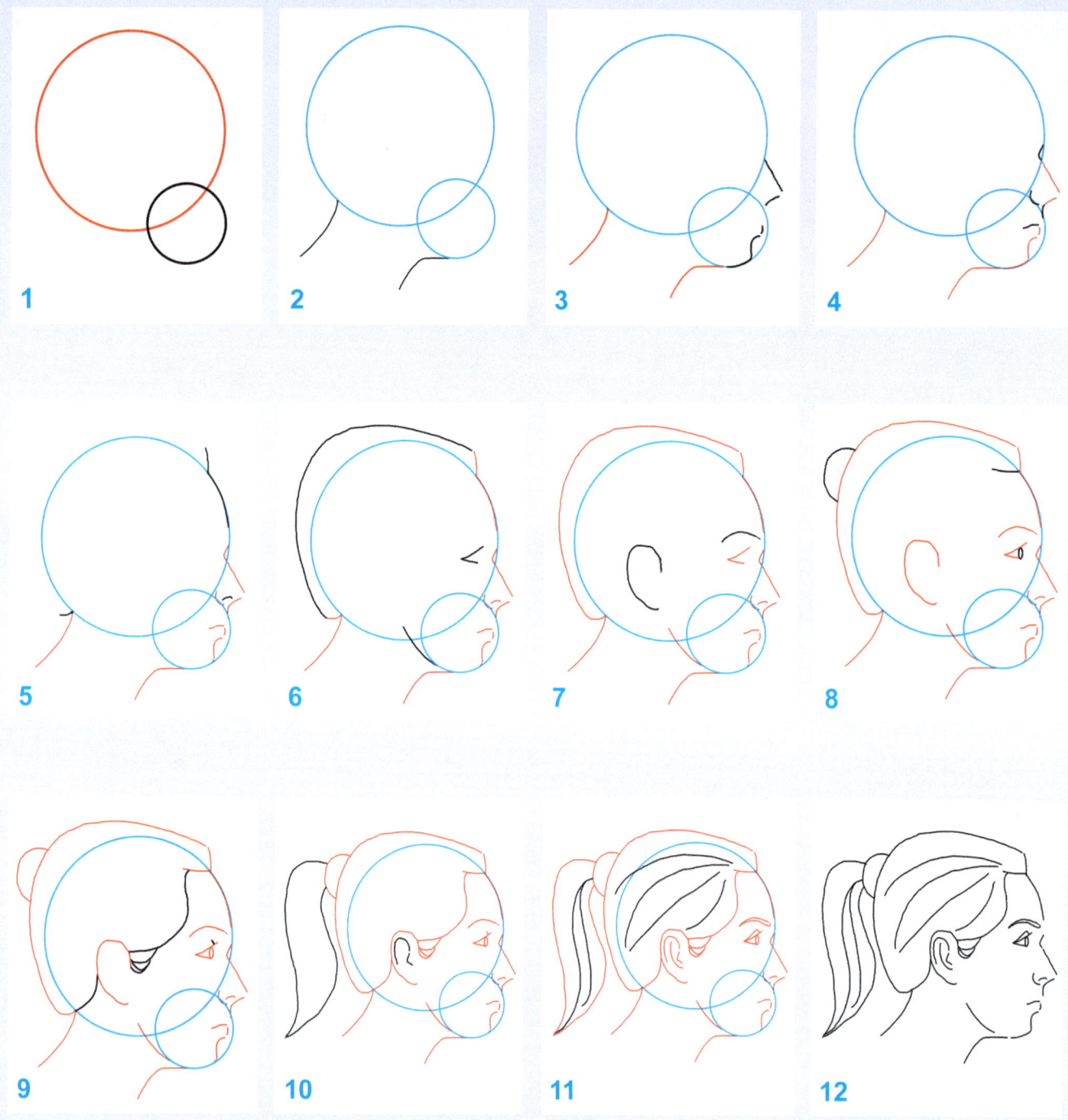

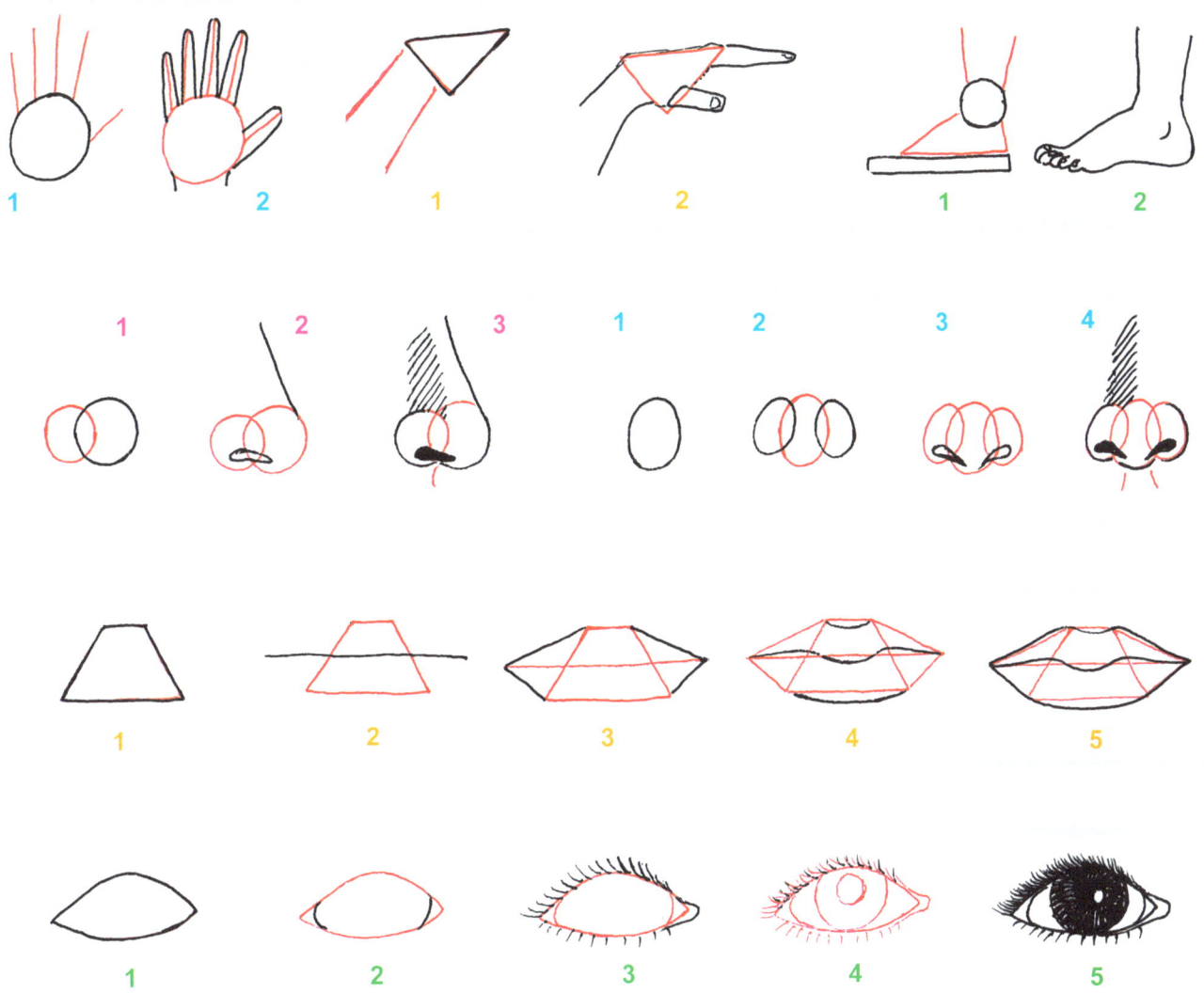

Up to this point, we have presented basics of visual arts, especially easy drawing (using shapes and simple lines). The models in this book are simple samples for teaching. So they can design any model they wish by using our method.

Color in nature

LSun is the source of color in nature. Scientists have that sun rays are a combination of 7 shades .

Que son : Violet , indigo , blue , green , yellow , orange and red .

These seven shades are the sources of other colors in nature and the sun light is a combination of all

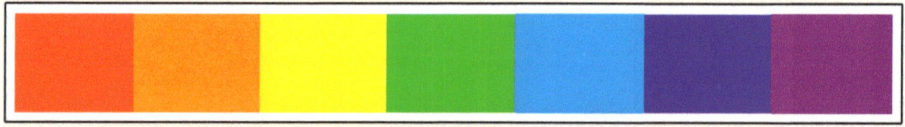

The seven color shade

Color in coloring

When we hear the word painting, the first thing that comes across our mind is color . Color is the main element of painting and coloring, without it, painting has no meaning The difference between a drawing and a painting is in the color . Drawing is like black and white picture but painting has color variety , like a color picture .

Colors are categorized in three groups :
primary, secondary and tertiary .

Primary colors :
Yellow, red and blue. Other colors are made of the combination of these three .
But they themselves cannot be made by mixing other colors .

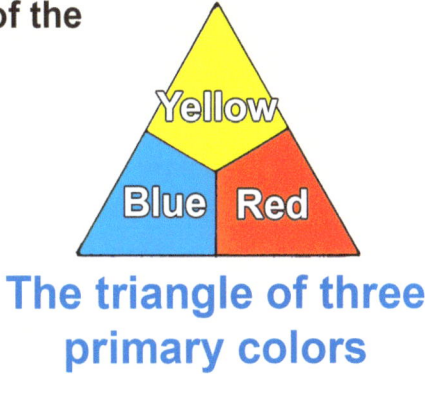

The triangle of three primary colors

Secondary colors :
By mixing yellow and blue we have green .
By mixing yellow and red we have orange
and by mixing blue and red we have purp
The new colors are called secondary color

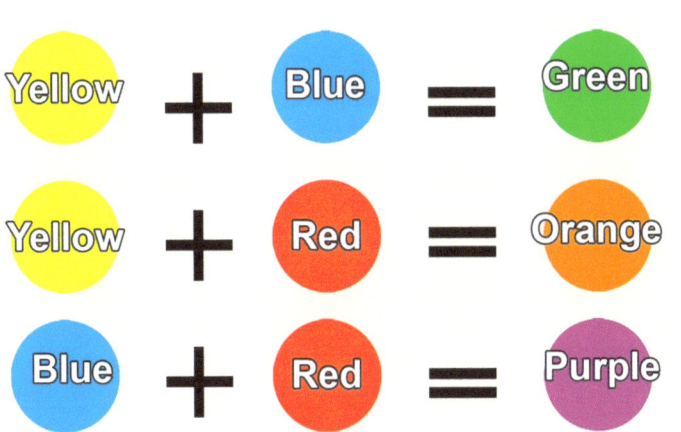

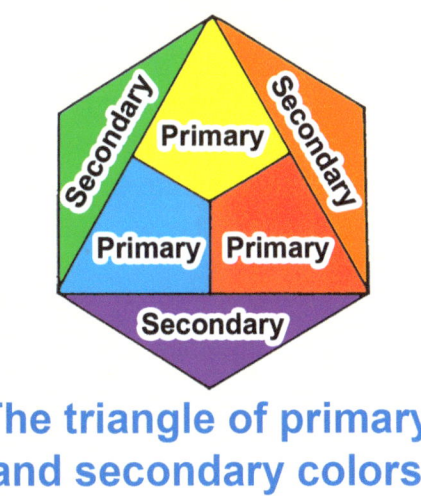

The triangle of primary and secondary colors

Tertiary Colors : When mixing two secondary colors one color is dominant that color is known as tertiary color. In the color circle that color is between a primary and secondary color such as: Red orange- Red yellow, purple red- Purple blue .

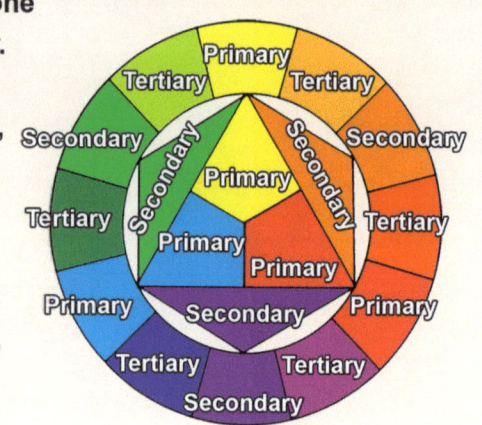

The complete circle and triangle of primary , secondary and tertiary

Additive and subtractive colors mixture :
If the three primary colors are mixed in equal portions, the color would be grey and the result is subtractive primary mixing . The combination of three primary color is called subtractive color mixture combination of lights of different perceived colors is called additive color mixture.
We are focusing on subtractive primary mixture and shall briefly go through it .

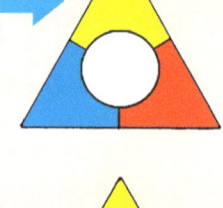

additive color miture
Color ray combination
primary color

Central subtractive color :
If three primary colors are mixed in equal portions, the combination is central subtractive mixture which is same as complete subtractive mixture .

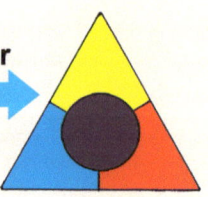

Central subtractive color
Three primary
color combination

None central subtractive mixture :
If in a combination one or two colors are mixed in more or lesser portions, that combination shall be a none central subtractive mixture and the color shall tend to be towards the one with most portion .

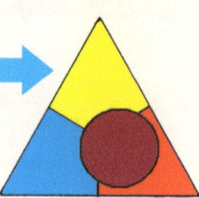

None central
subtractive mixture
Three primary
color combination

Grey color (1) : If in a none central mixture, a color tends towards one or two color, the result shall be grey color.

Grey color (2) : By mixing black and white and another color of the color circle, a different grey will be created.

Complementary colors : If any two primary colors are in a combination, the missing third color shall be the complementary color.

Two complementary colors are in contrast to each other.

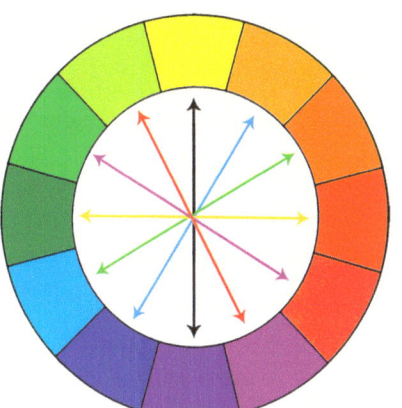

In the color circle, the complementary colors (Contrasting colors) are exactly opposite each other

Grey is the result of mixing black and white. If any other color of the color circle is added to black and white, a different shade of grey is achieved.

Warm colors : Warm colors are any color combination in which any of the three yellow, red and orange are dominant because they convey warmth to a viewer.

Cool colors : Cool colors are any color combination in which any of the two, green and blue are dominant because they make the viewer feel cool.

Painting with cool colors

Painting with warm colors

Warm colors cause excitement activity, anxiety and violence in the viewer and they are also appetizing but cool colors make the viewer feel calm and less active.

In this section in order to encourage using coloring pencils, we shall focus on very simple methods . You shall see how easy it is to use coloring pencils directly. The student shall find them very enjoyable to work with, you should keep in mind that any work may seem hard at first but if it's done with a little accuracy and analysis, it will be much easier than what it appeared first, and of course that is if it's done in proper and reasonable way

We shall now start coloring with pencils in an easy method .

Pencil tip **Using the side of the pencil lead** **Stippling**

It must be mentioned that the above techniques are not the only methods of using the color pencils ; as you grow more experienced and skillful , there will be many more which you can use .

Hatching

Según el tejido del modelose puede utilizar de los cuatros métodos para colorearlo .Utilizar el lápiz de color no límite a cuatro métodos sino con lograr más experiencias lograrán aplicaciones más diversas .

1 2 3 4

52

1 2 3 4

1 2 3 4

53

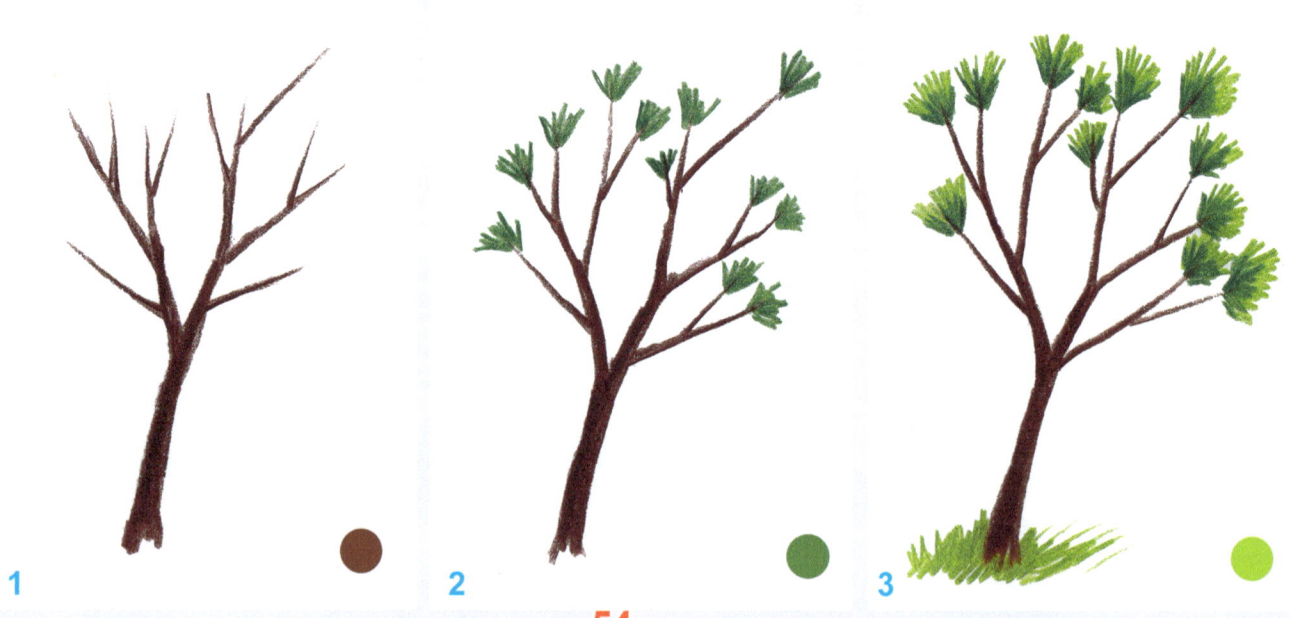

1 2 3 4 5

1 2 3 4 5

1

2

3

1

2

3

4

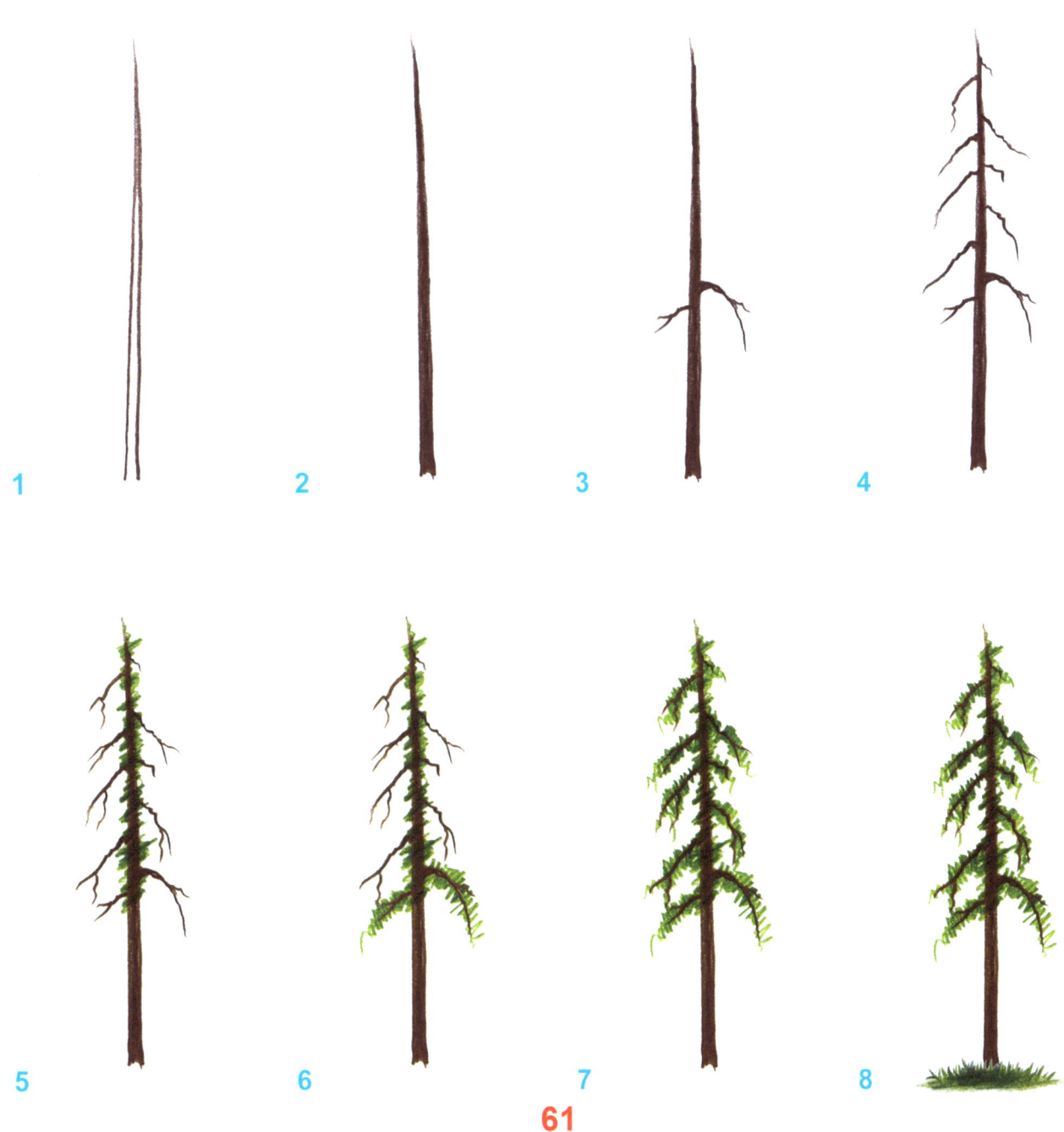

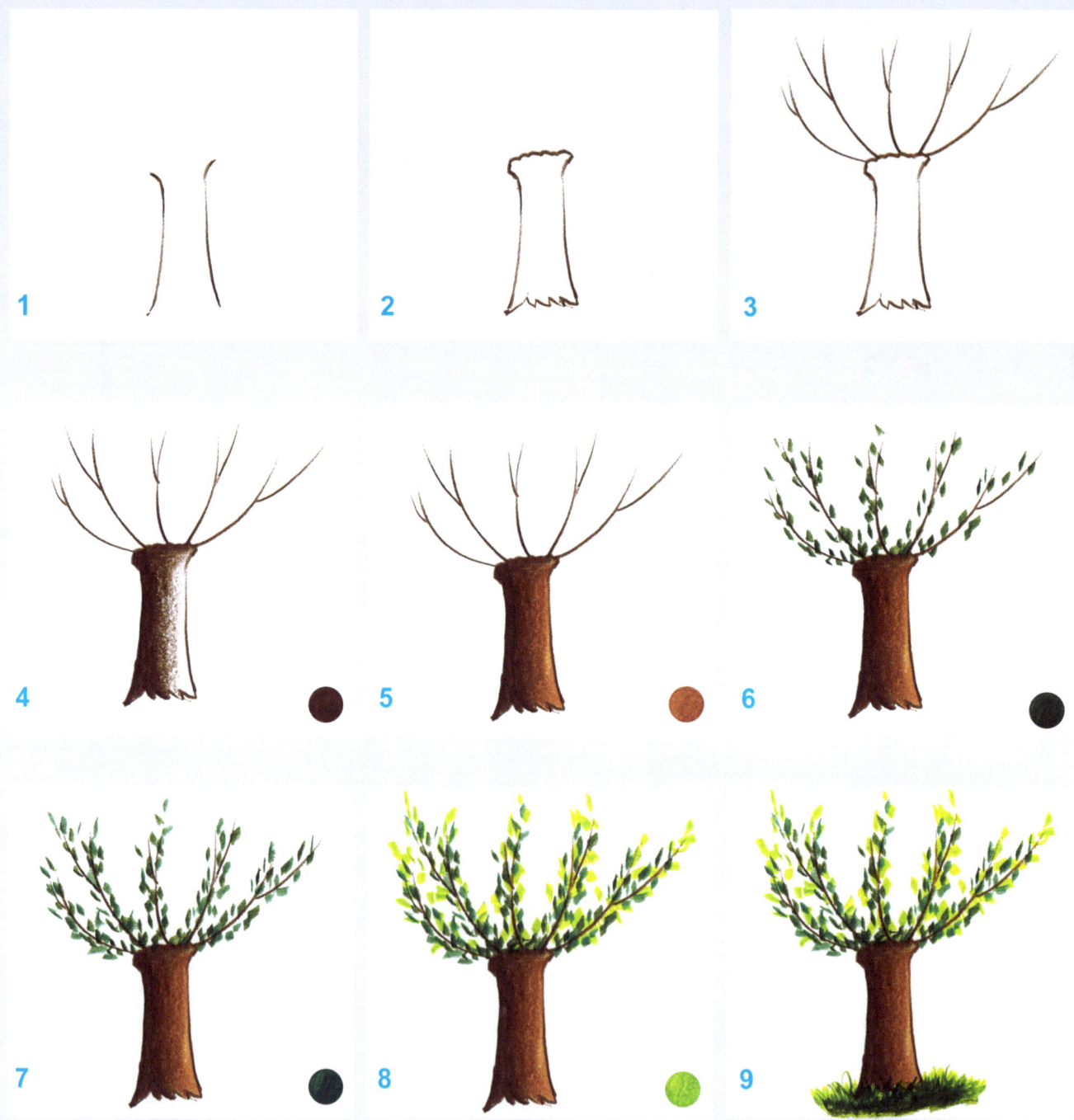

1　　　　　2　●　　　　3　●　　●

4　　●　　5　　●　　6　　●

63

1 2  3 4 5 6

64

65

1

2

3

4

67

Considering the facts that distant things are smaller, their color fade and they seem blur and as they get closer, they become bigger , more clear and colors are richer (in order to have a more natural looking painting we should follow the above points)

70

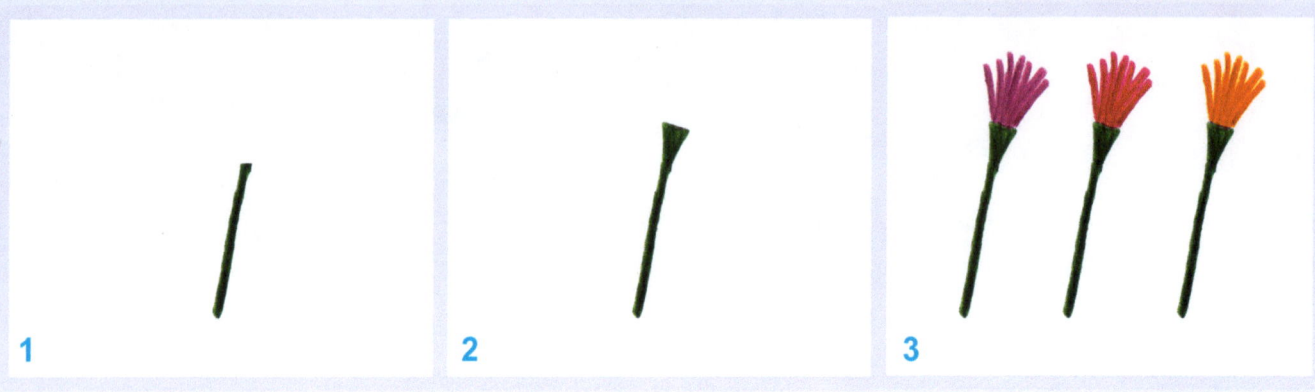

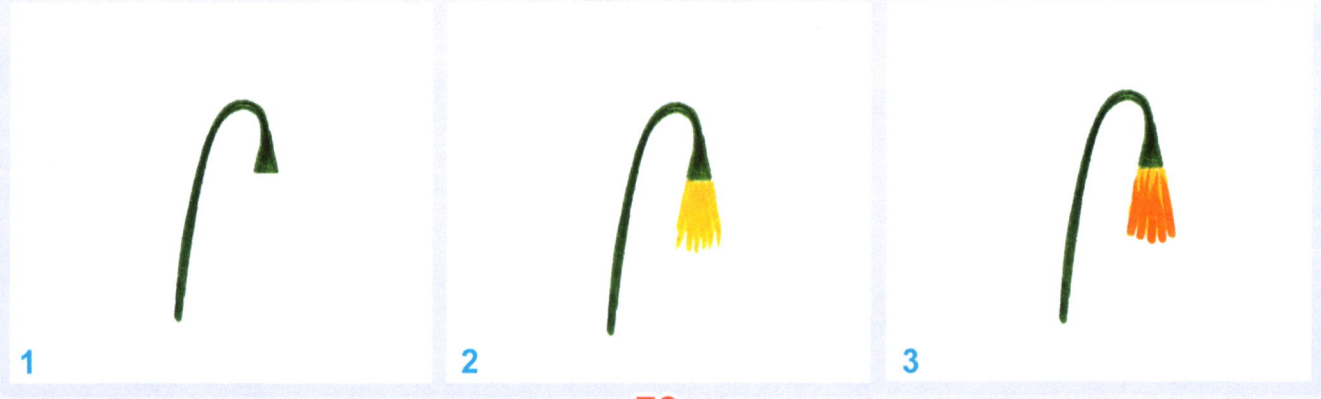

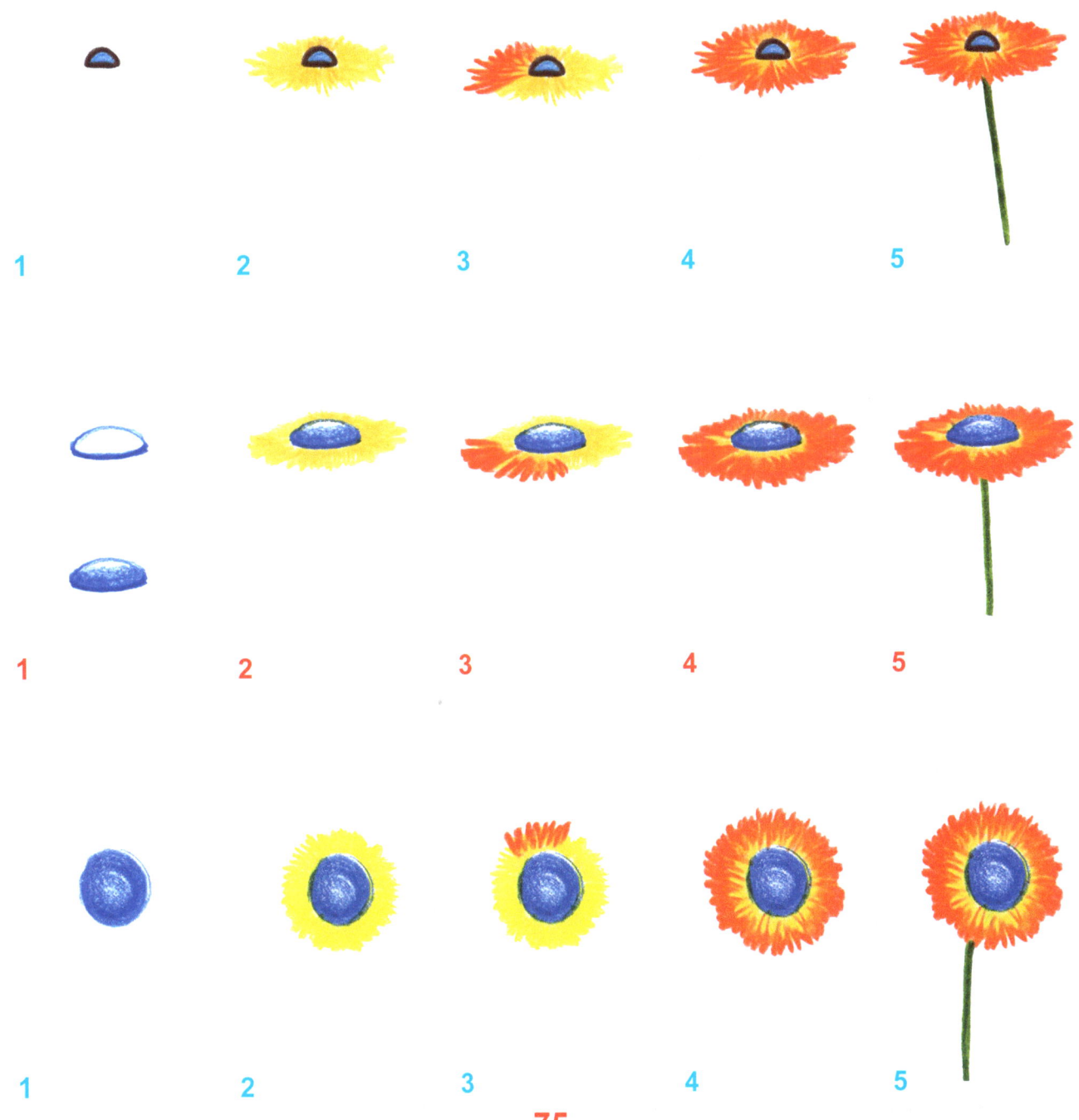

 1
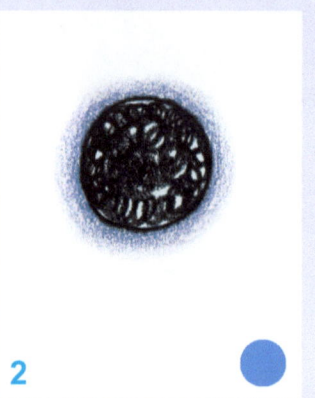 2
 3
 4

 1
 2
 3
 4

 1
 2
 3
 4

78

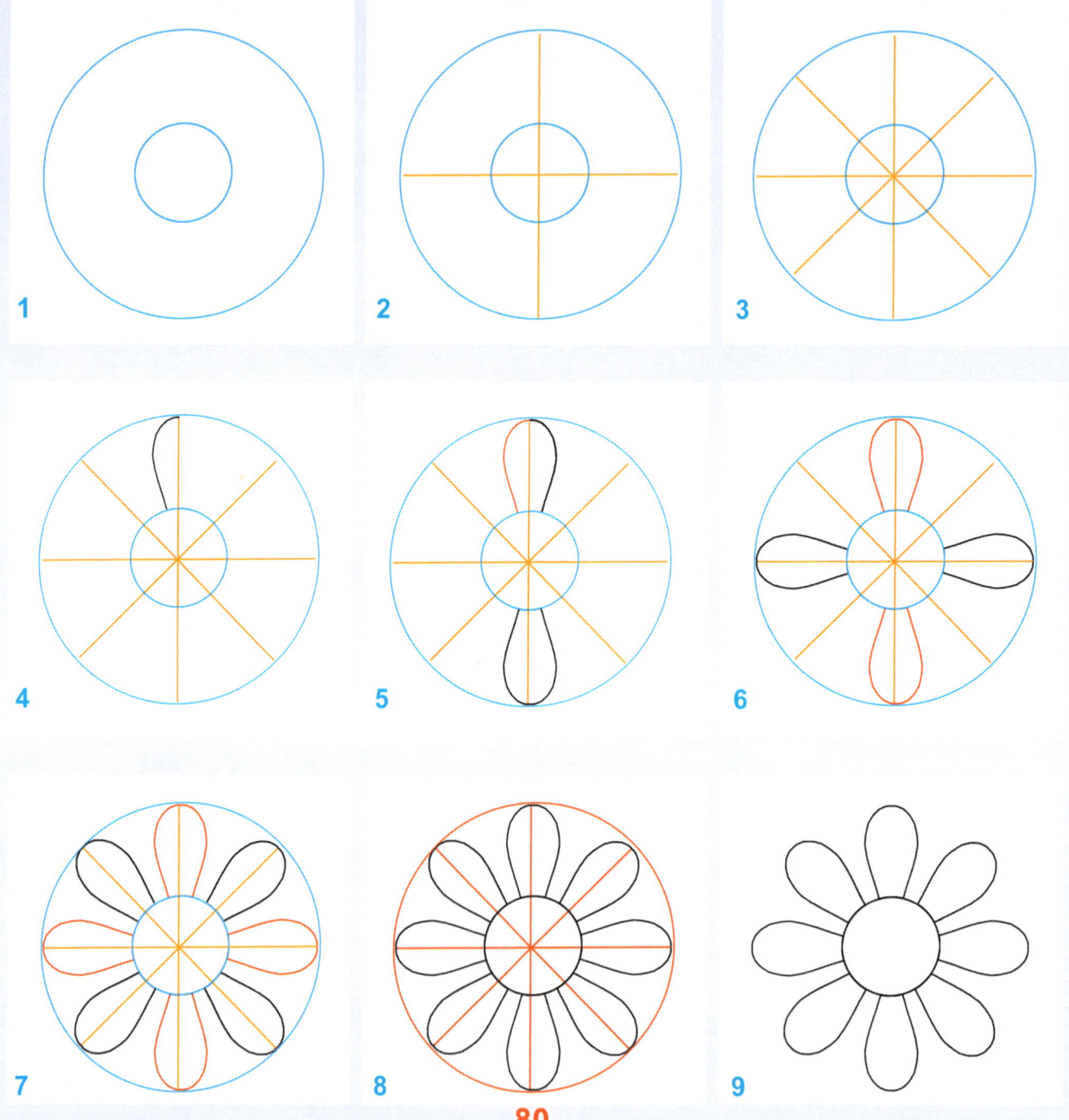

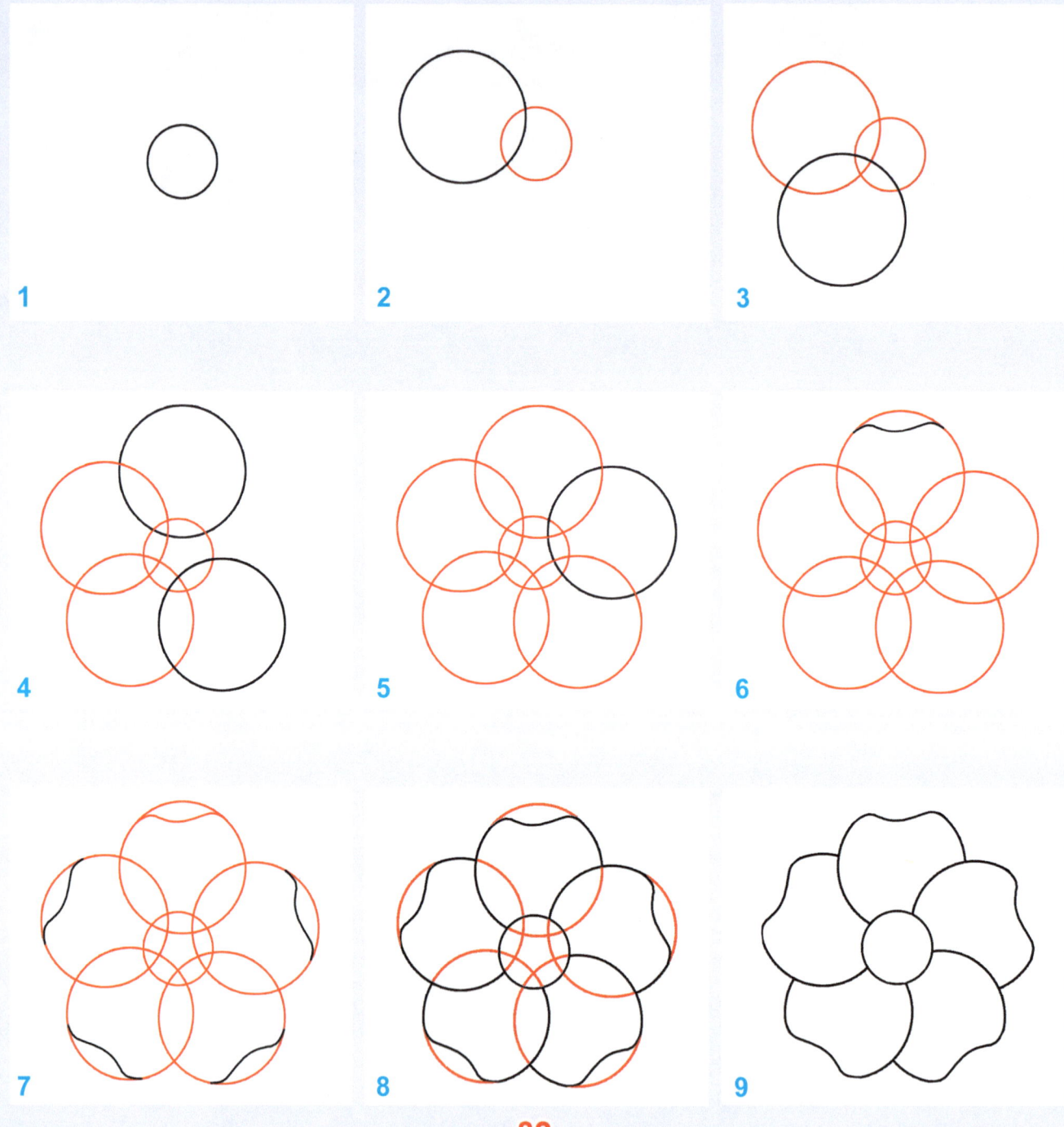

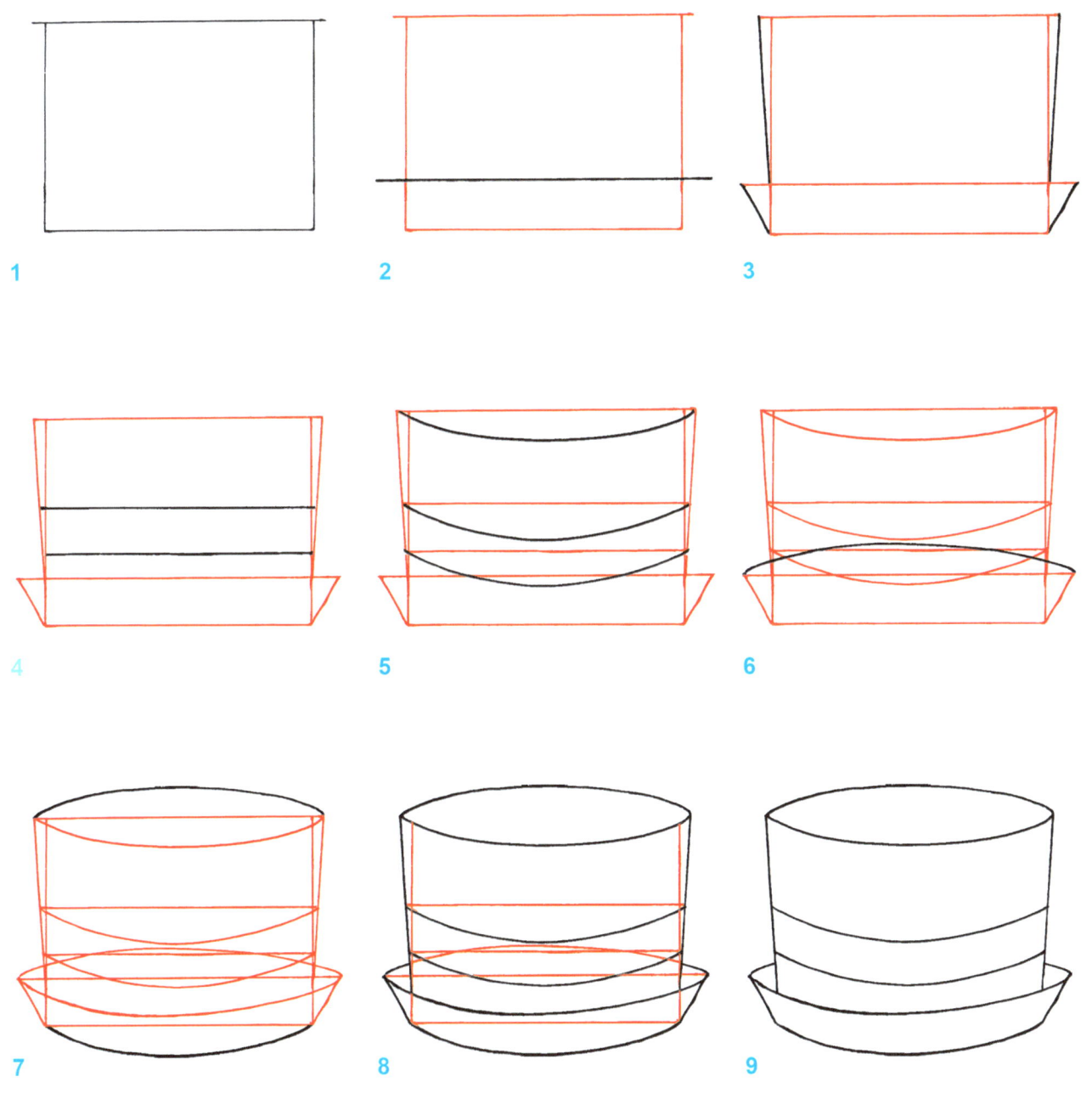

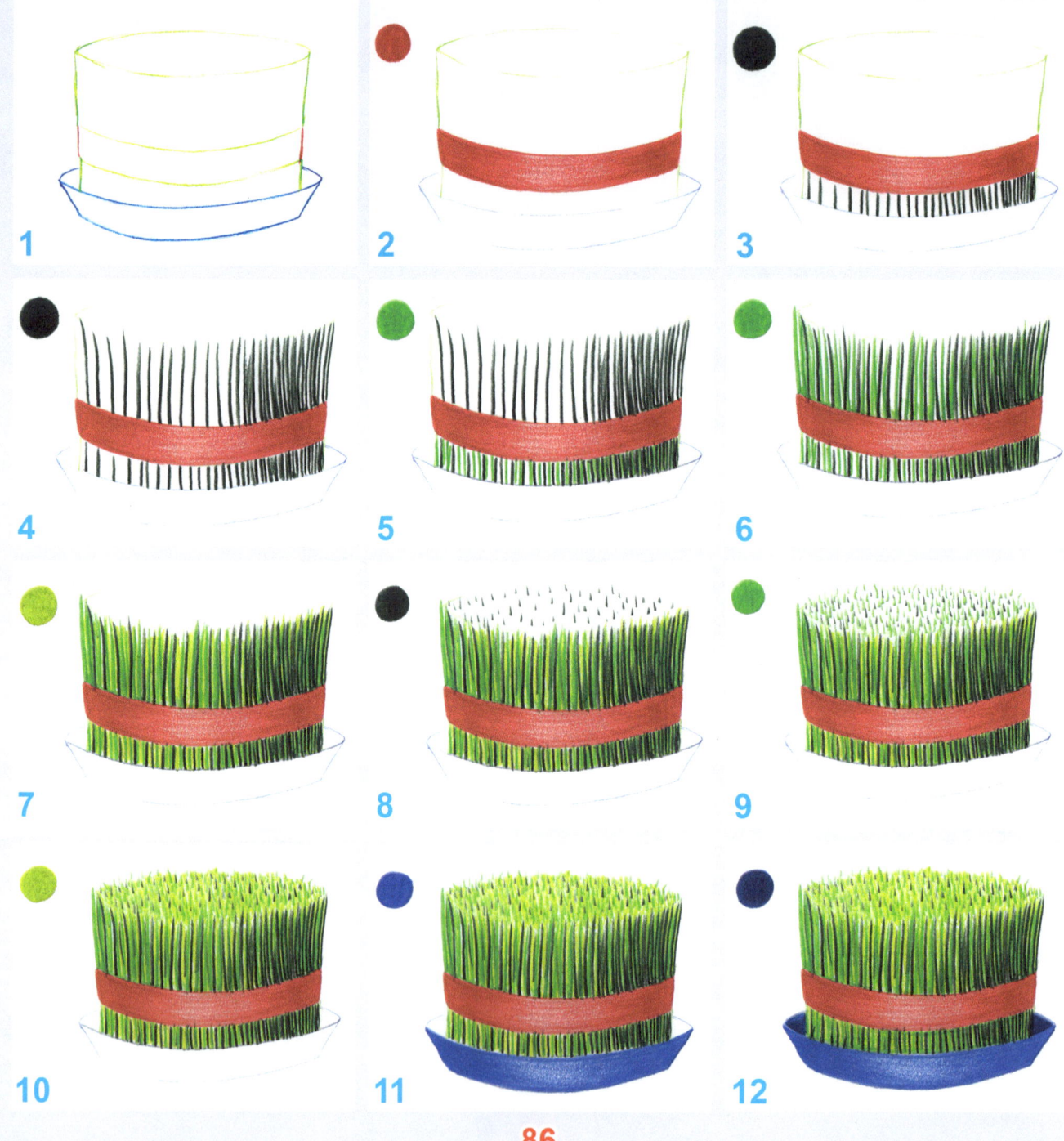

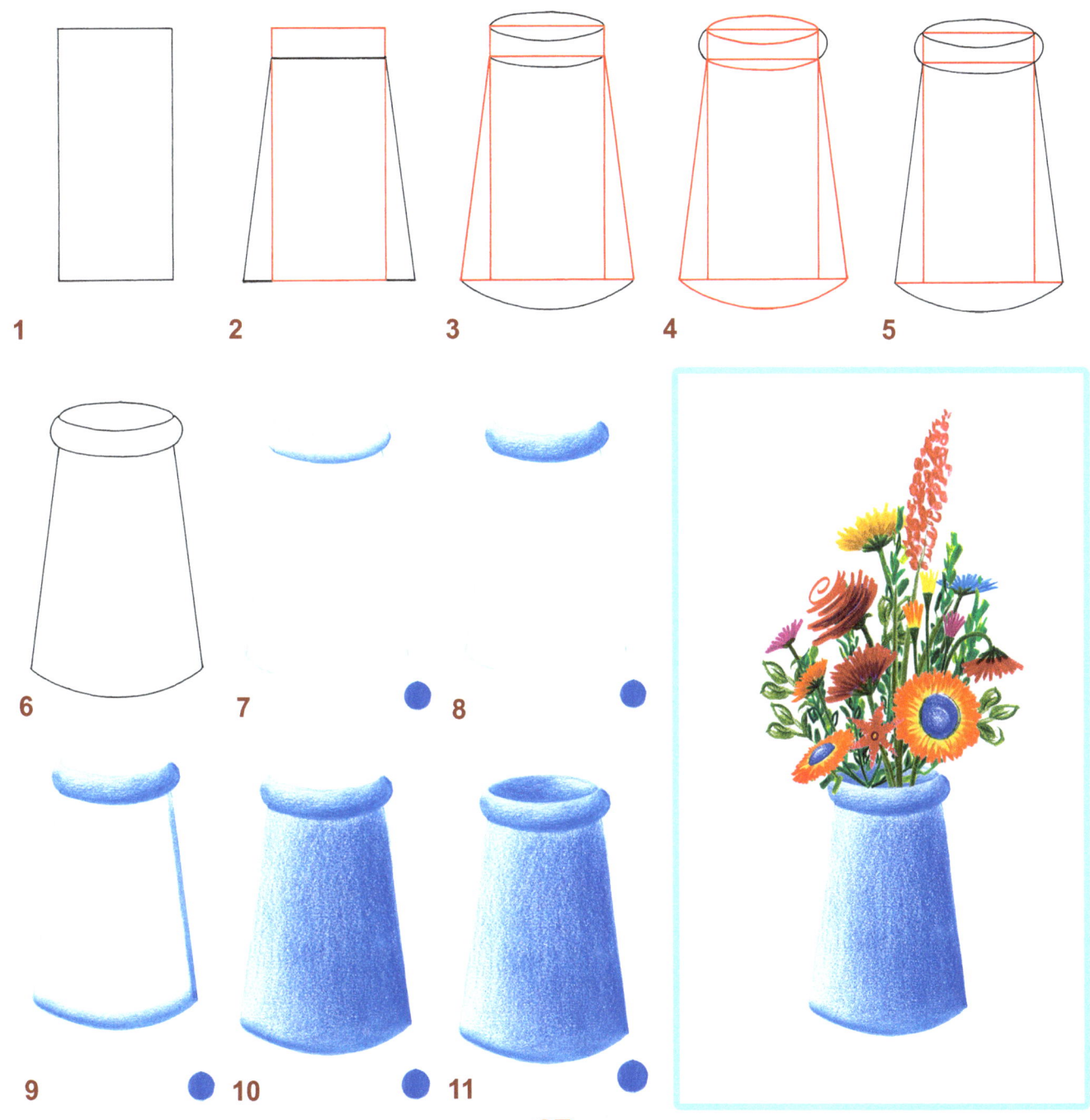

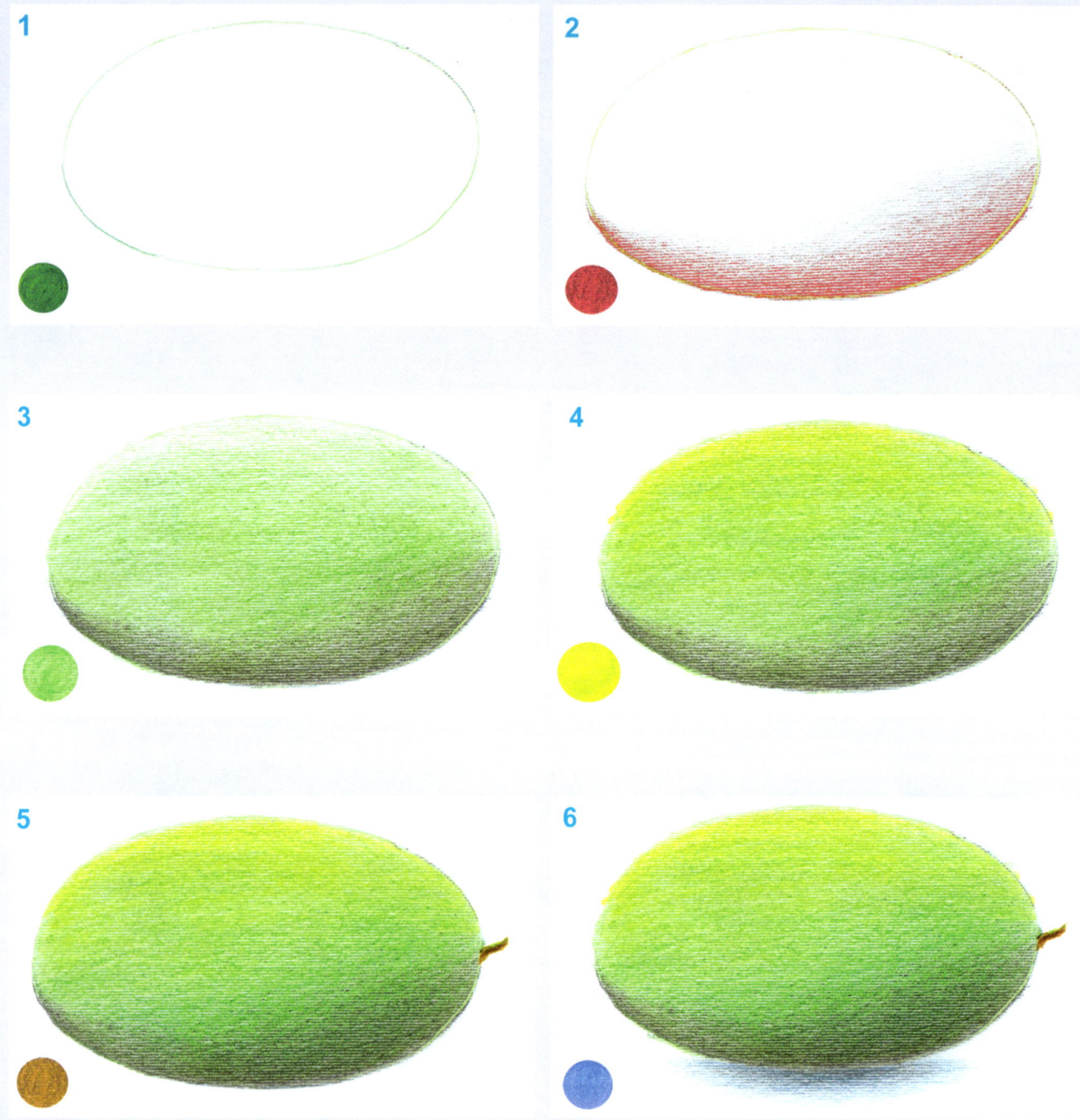

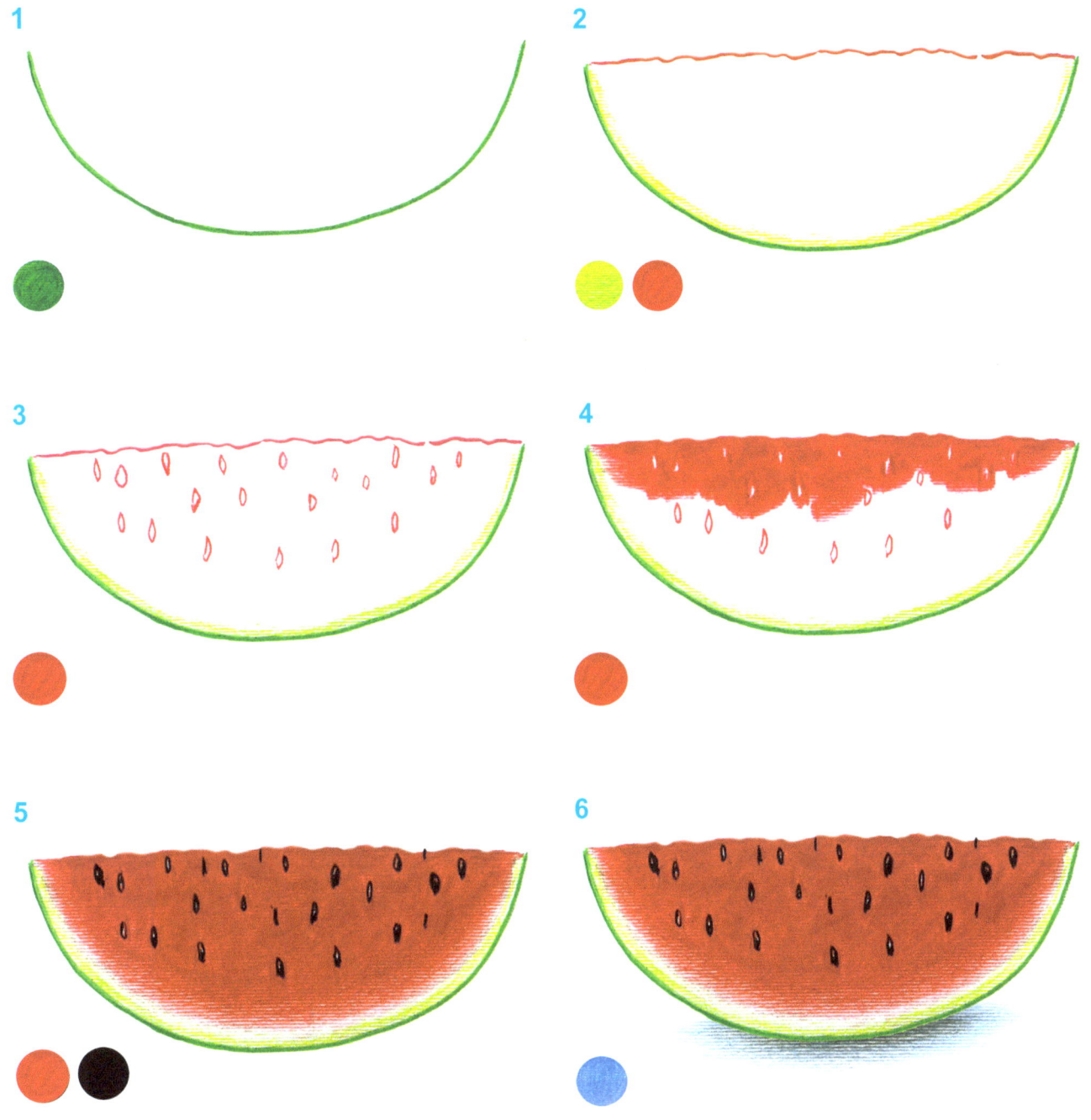

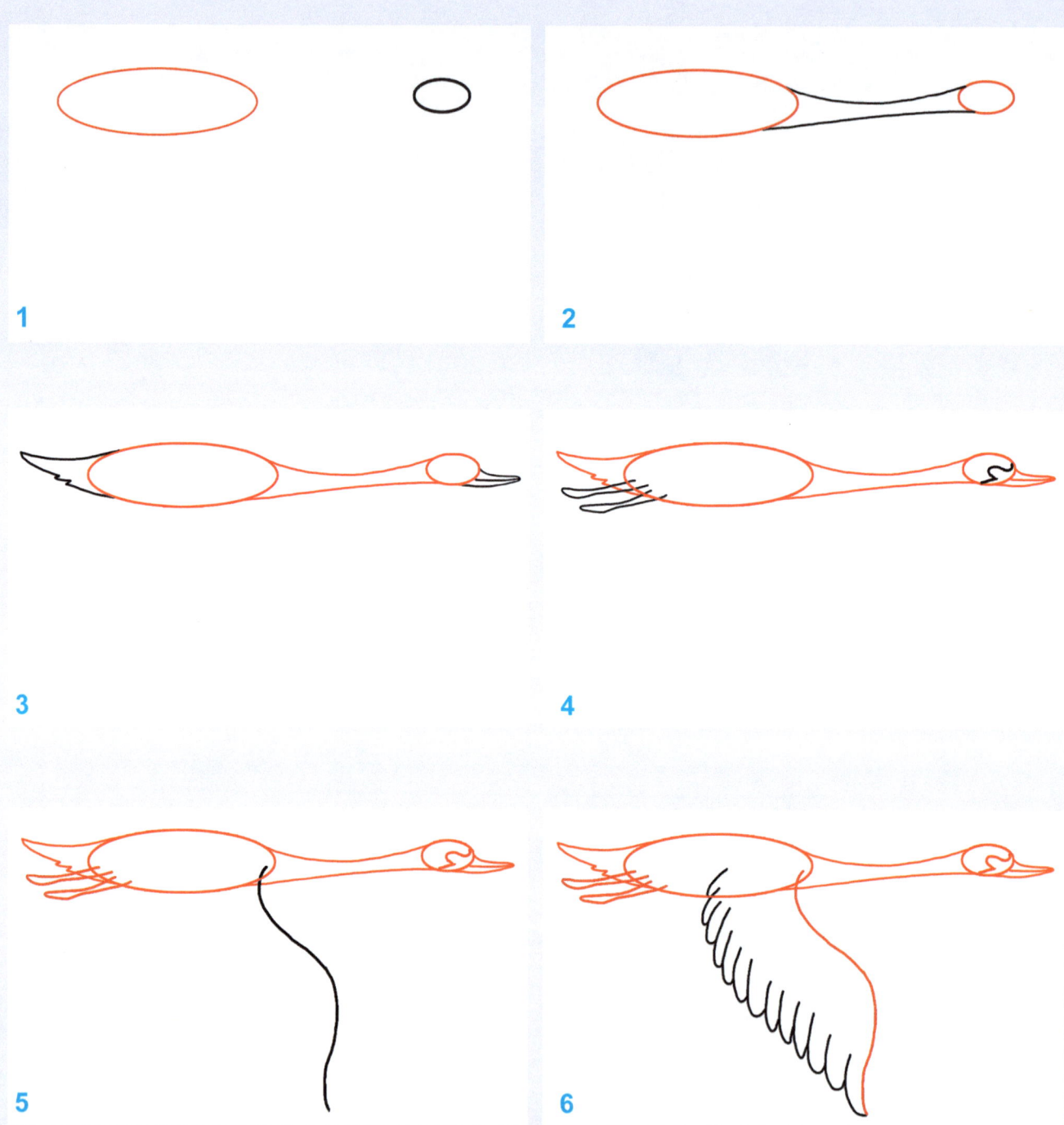

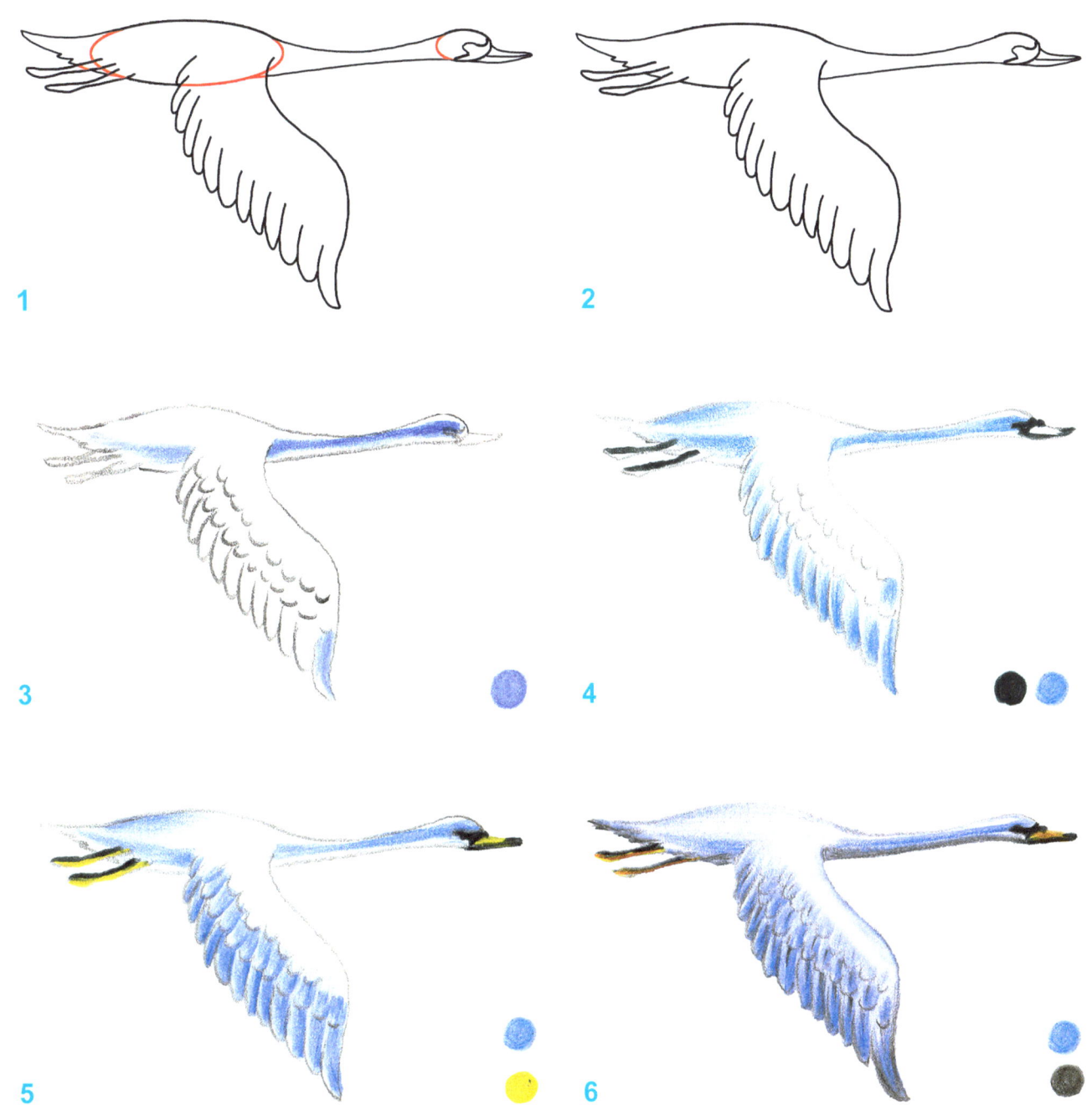

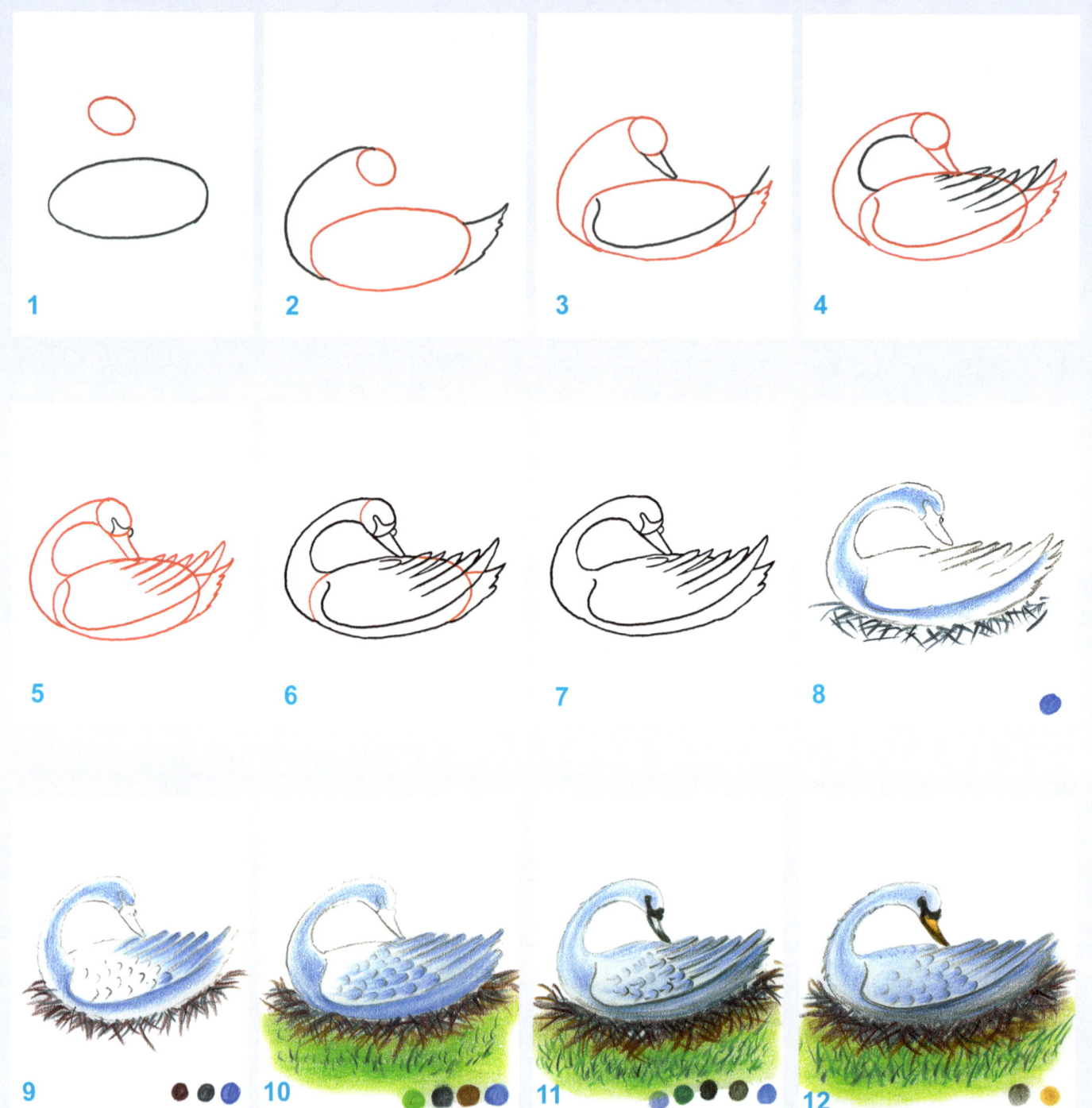

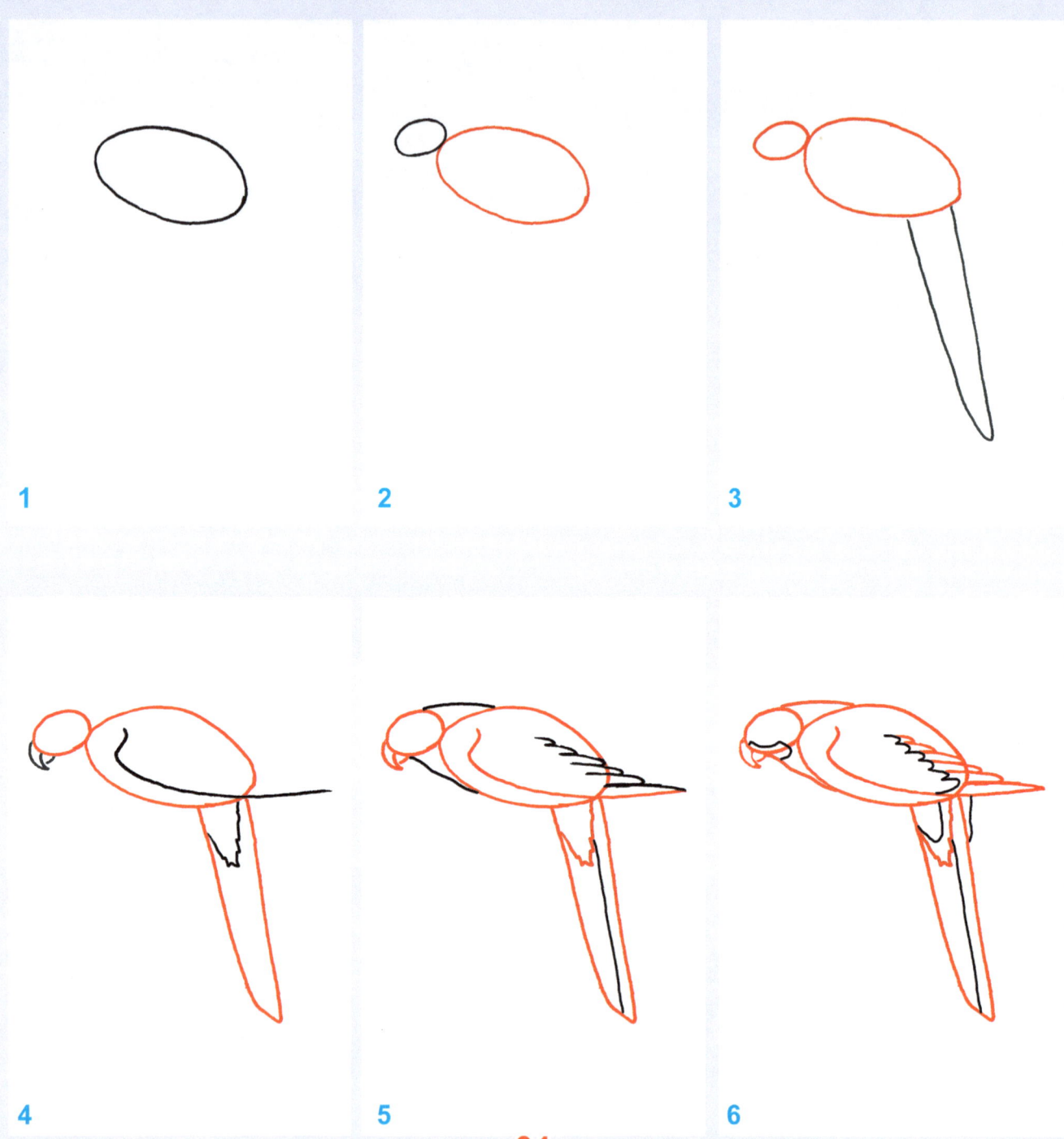

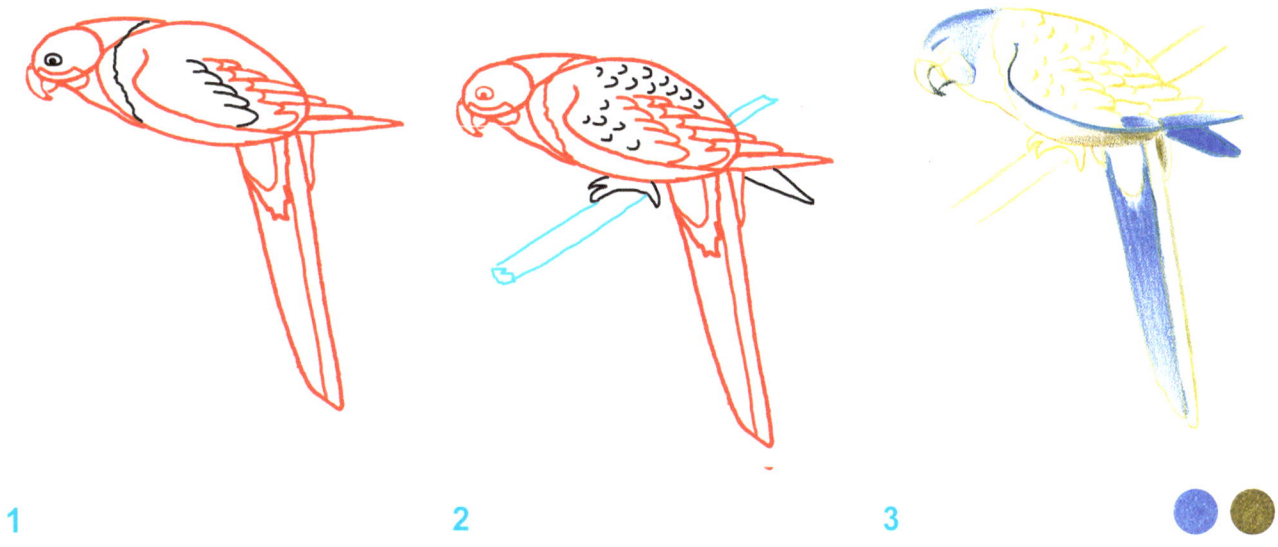

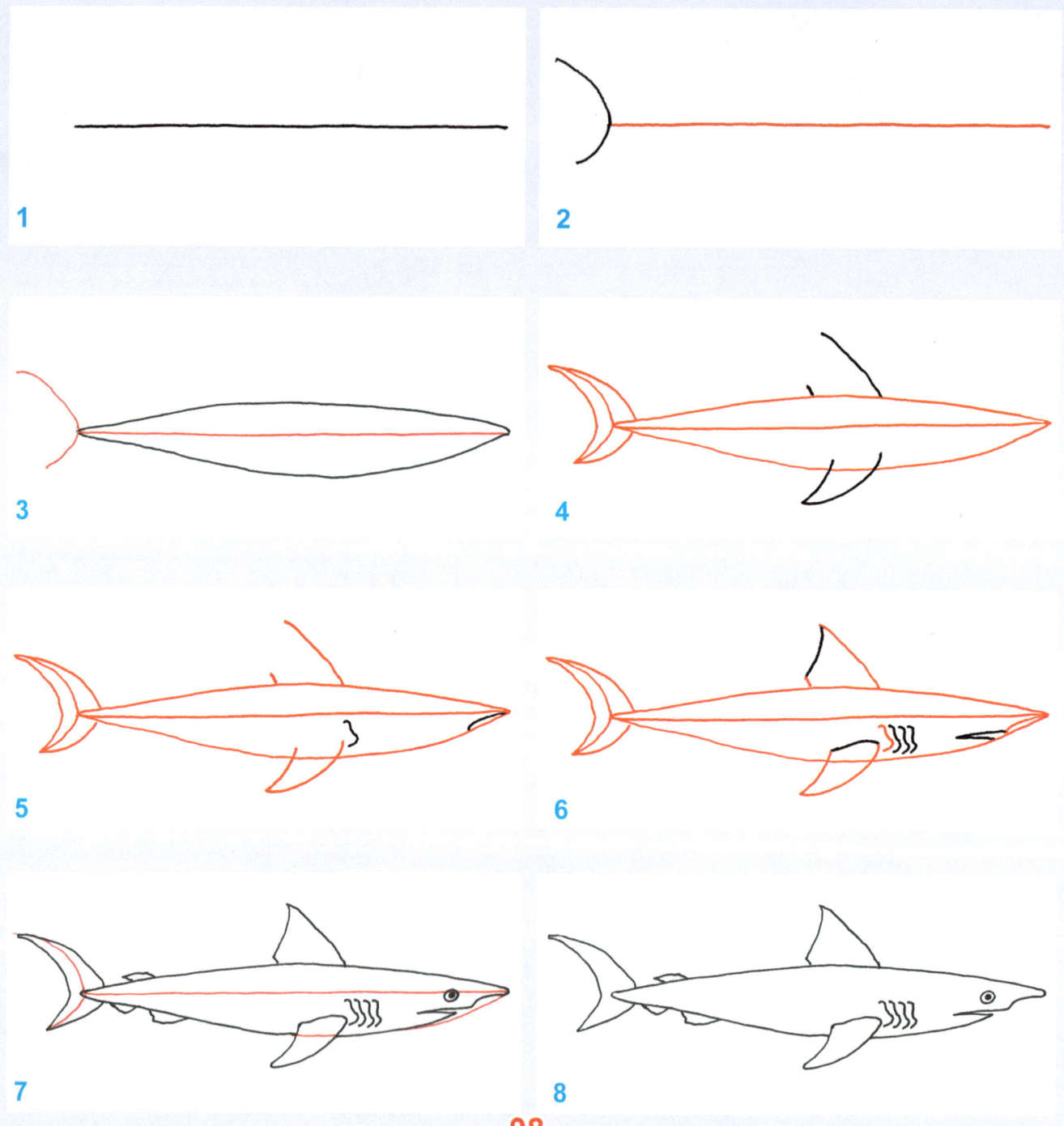

99

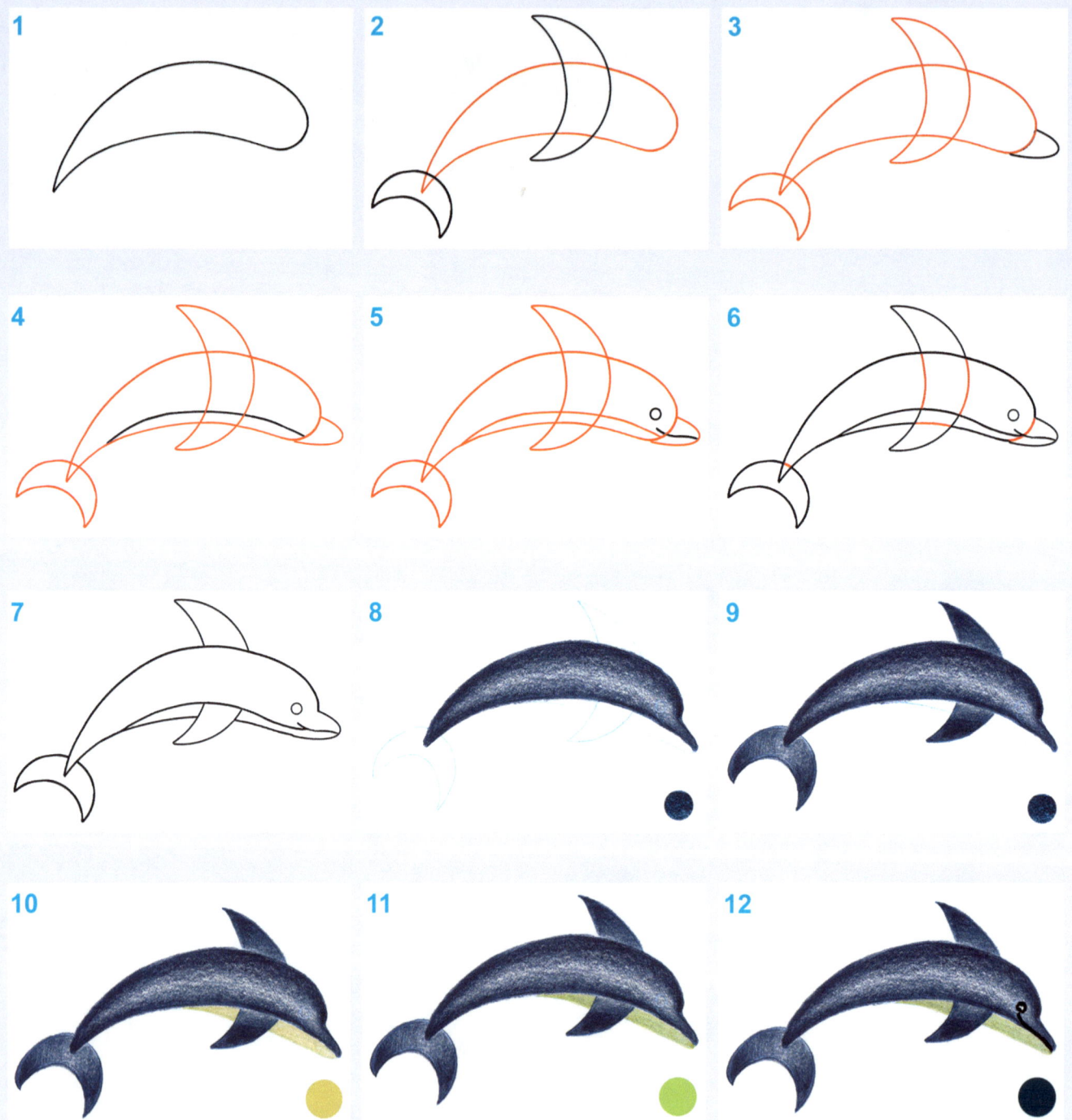

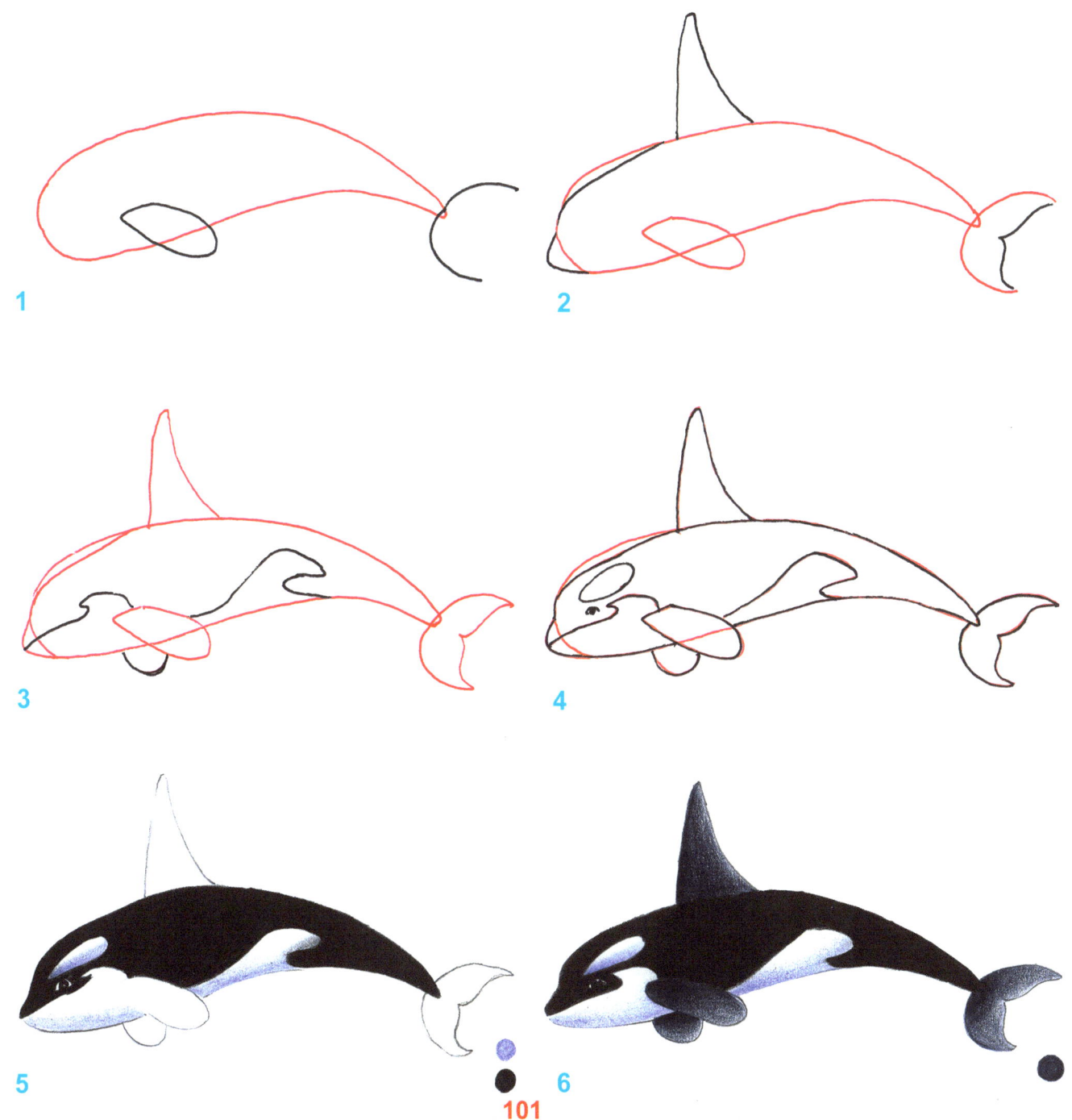

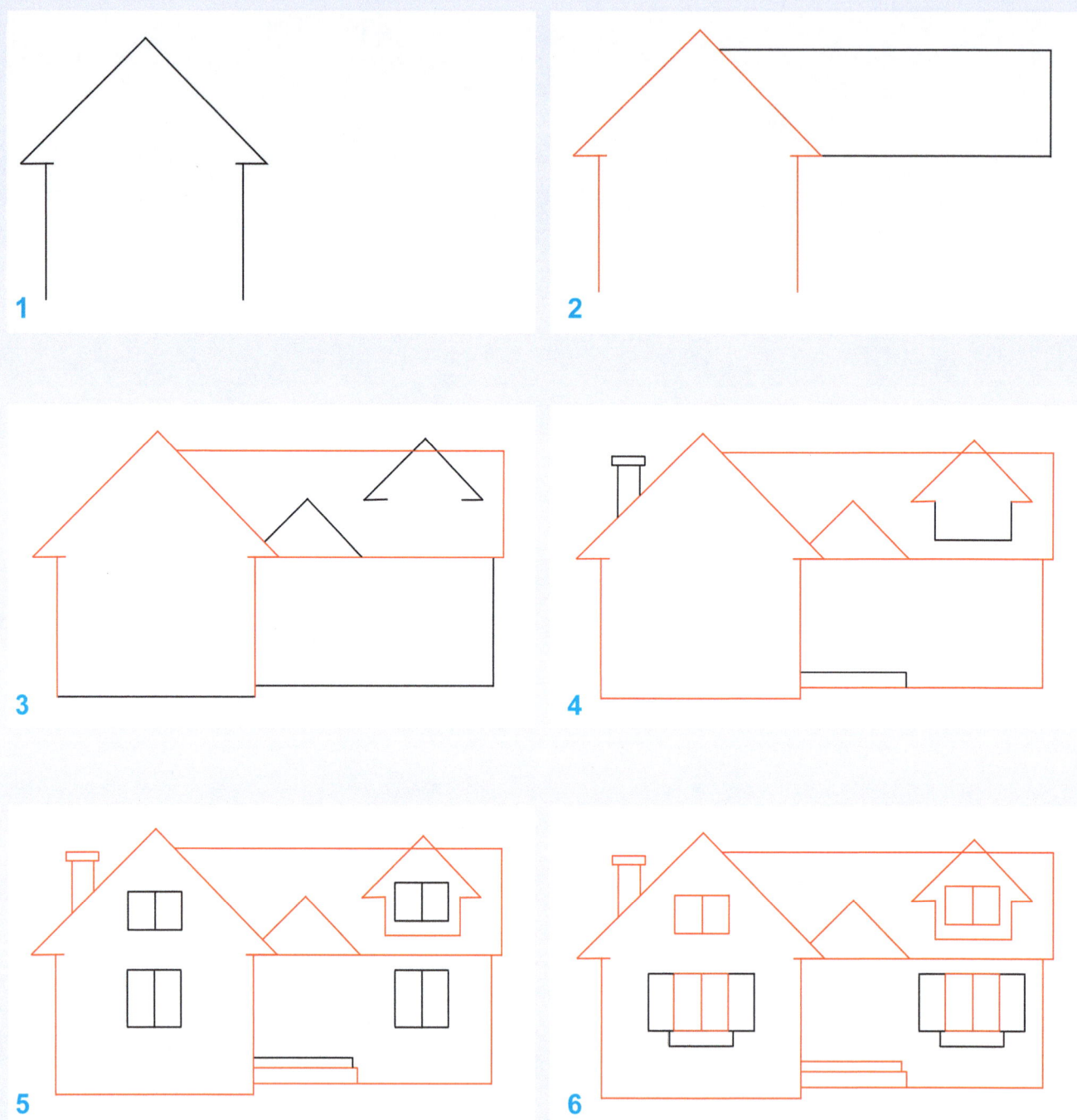

13

14

15

16 16

17

18

19

105

Author's forward

The ability to do something fast and carefully is called skill while art is creativity and innovation in every skill which is in the path of perfection! Therefore, the prerequisite and prior condition of art is being skillful. To motivate our children and beginners to show creativity and innovation, the new generation should be taught some special skills . In Sana series we have tried to make learning drawing , painting , and similar skills easy through applying mathematical simplification .

Sana Books Series and the applied method are the result of 30-year creative experience of the author who has not plagiarized from any sources.
In fact, they are based on the author's experimental and individual thought which have been systematically presented .

teaching Art to children and adolescents using simplification
(the same one used in mathematics), Sana book series seriously focuses on motivation and other goals, meaning improving general abilities in the new generation :

Some of the general goals of Sana Art teaching are: internalizing mental and behavioral discipline along with improving concentration, self-confidence and self-esteem. Increasing positive imagination, improving the compatibility between mind and the hand, and boosting the threshold of tolerance are the other goals of the series .

Art is the best method and tool to improve the general abilities and talents of children and adolescents. If it is applied consciously and wisely, it will have marvelous results. Drawing and painting, because of paying step by step attention to the process , would improve the general abilities in children .

The steps in painting and drawing : **1 - observing   2 - memorizing   3 - depicting**

1 - observing : As the required observation in drawing is accompanied with precision and a high level of concentration, it is per se an efficient exercise to increase precision and concentration in children .

2 - memorizing : Due to the improvement of conscious imagination in the second step (memorizing) , the ability of memorizing in children is naturally improved. It means the brain is getting sharper in learning .

3 - depicting : In the third step, drawing and painting (depicting) cause an intimate relationship between the brain and hand, leading into the ability to create handicrafts in children .

Relying on experiences and effectively, it has been consciously and wisely attempted to observe the following issues in Sana Training books .

In Sana book series of teaching Art, we follow the goals according to the interest and willingness in children and adolescents . We hope the desired improvement and development can help all the children from various ethnicities and nationalities to reach the top of salvation and redemption .

After acknowledging the positive and helpful effects of Sana Books , we hope you are motivated to provide the other books of the series so that the educational plans will be more effectively achieved in your dear children .

The other works published by the author ("Sana" Art Training Books)

Sana
Basic Drawing and Painting Exercises
" for children between 2 - 5 years old"
(The first step in drawing and painting)
These are some exercises to improve
the relationship between the mind
and hand. These exercises enable the
hand to depict whatever the brain images

Painting with **Sana** colorful collage papers : landscaping volume 1
Deals with making illustrations, using colorful collage papers, scissors, and glue

Painting with **Sana** colorful collage papers : landscaping volume 2
Deals with making illustrations, using colorful collage papers, scissors, and glue

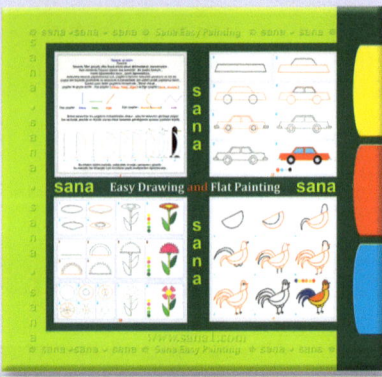

Sana
Easy Drawing and Flat Painting
(applying the simplest technique)
By using Sana Series of Teaching
Art, everybody at every age can
teach himself drawing and painting
A colorful 108- page book in quarto
24/5×22/5

Sana
Teaching Painting and Drawing
(applying the simplest technique)
volume 1
By using the book, you can be your painting teacher of yours and others
A colorful 108- page book in quarto
24/5×22/5

Sana
Teaching Painting and Drawing
(applying the simplest technique)
volume 2
After practicing based on the first volume, the second one can enable everybody to paint framable artistic paintings
A colorful 108 - page book in quarto
24/5×22/5

WWW.ART-SANA.COM

www.ingramcontent.com/pod-product-compliance
Lightning Source LLC
Chambersburg PA
CBHW042016150426
43197CB00002B/46